Programs for Advent and Christmas

VOLUME III

Edited by Elizabeth Wright Gale

Judson Press ® Valley Forge

116696

Copyright © 1989
Judson Press, Valley Forge, PA 19482-0851

Unless otherwise indicated, Bible quotations in this volume are from the Revised Standard Version of the Bible, copyrighted 1946, 1952, © 1971, 1973 by the Division of Christian Education of the National Council of the Churches of Christ in the U.S.A., and used by permission.

Other quotations of the Bible are from the *Good News Bible*, the Bible in Today's English Version. Copyright © American Bible Society, 1976. Used by permission.

Library of Congress Cataloging-in-Publication Data

Programs for Advent and Christmas / Elizabeth Wright Gale, editor.
    p. cm.
    ISBN 0-8170-1149-8 : $6.95
    1. Christmas. 2. Advent. 3. Christmas plays, American.
  1. Gale, Elizabeth Wright.
  BV45.P76 1989
  263'.91—dc20   89-15486
                                             CIP

Table of Contents

What If—? I Wonder . . .

by Gracie McCay

What if—
I sent no Christmas cards this year?
I did not bake Christmas cookies or candy?
I made each of my Christmas gifts especially for the person receiving it?
I gave only one gift to each member of my family? (Yes, to the children, too!)
I decided to give a special segment of time in the coming year to those persons important to me?
I didn't feel I *had* to entertain groups of friends and family?
I took time really to listen to great Christmas music?
I participated in and exchanged Christmas traditions with persons from another ethnic group?
I didn't *feel obligated* to attend certain holiday events or parties?
I shared my Christmas dinner with those who are truly hungry?
I gave gifts to charitable causes in the names of those to whom I usually give gifts?
I did not go Christmas shopping?
I receive gifts from those to whom I do not give?
What if—?

I wonder . . .
Would the spirit of Christmas be able to find its expression through me?
Would my senses be aware of needs of persons around me?
Would I be open and free to give of myself and to receive others?
Would the star of Bethlehem shine more brightly?
Would the angels' message come clearer?
Would I find my way to the manger with the shepherds?
Would I "travel as far" as the wise men traveled to give a gift of love?
Would the Christ child's birth become vivid— surround me with awe?
Would joy fill my life and touch others?
Would I find the path to peace within myself and with others?
Would Christmas truly happen?

What if—? I wonder . . .

From Shopping Mall to Sanctuary

An Advent Values Experience for Youth or Adults

by Julia Bebeau

It happens every year. As December nears, we all know that we'll get caught by it in some way: the Christmas Crunch. Cards to write, gifts to buy and wrap and mail, goodies to bake, parties and church functions and school programs to attend—the list goes on and on, and with it comes a mounting anxiousness. We all know it steals the true spirit of Christmas. Yet, year after year it happens.

Advent—the season of waiting and preparing for the coming of the Messiah, the Christ child,

Joe Tritsch

Immanuel, God with us here and now. The wonder of God's coming to us in the form of that tiny, very human baby, the essence of the gospel, captures us all. Our traditions add to the meaning of the season and enrich our experience of it. They draw us together as friends and as family. Persons reach out to one another with a warmth not seen or felt at other times of the year. So, where does the Christmas Crunch fit in? Is this what we associate with Advent, those holy weeks leading up to Christmas? Could it be that in those weeks the crunch overshadows the crèche?

Here is an active Advent experience designed to assist youth or adults in sorting through their values at this season. It focuses on the contrast between the Christmas of the shopping mall and that of the sanctuary. It might be done on a Friday evening, a Saturday afternoon and evening, or even a Sunday. It will take a good chunk of time to allow for an outing as well as some activities back at the church, but the process is an essential part of the learning and promises to enrich the Advent experience of all who participate.

The Event—Part 1

Gather at the church and prepare to go to a nearby shopping mall or a downtown shopping area. If you live in a rural area, this may mean some travel, but that adds to the adventure, too. If your group is large, divide into smaller groups or have each person choose a partner for the outing. Then make the following assignments for each group or pair to accomplish.

1. Spend a half hour just walking and observing people, interactions, shopping styles, signs, and so forth.

2. Spend the next half hour taking notes about what you've seen and heard. In particular, deal with these questions:

- What are the key slogans? What are they saying about gift giving?
- What kinds of gifts are merchants "pushing" this year?
- What are the signs of Christmas here? What creates the magic?
- What kinds of interactions do you see between persons?

3. Spend the next half hour conducting "person-in-the-mall" / "person-on-the-street" interviews, asking some of the following questions:

- What do you enjoy most about this season?
- What concerns you most about this season?
- Do you enjoy shopping for friends, family? What kinds of gifts do you plan to give this year?
- How do you see the meaning of Christmas?
- Make up some of your own questions, too!

Encourage consideration and prudence in approaching interviewees. Suggest that persons introduce themselves and talk with people of all ages, even a clerk if they can find one free.

Gauge the time of each of the three assignments according to your schedule.

The Event—Part 2

Return to the church and have the participants go directly to the sanctuary (or wherever your church's center of Christmas celebration may be). Ask them to spend the next five to ten minutes sitting quietly, reflecting on the experience thus far, taking in the new surroundings. Then break the silence by reading the Christmas story as told in Luke 2:1–14.

Do some talking together about the Christmas traditions in your church. What are some of the signs of Christmas here? Ask them to relate some of their favorite Christmas memories and traditions associated with the church.

Now, do some debriefing about the mall or downtown experience. Ask for reports from their note taking and interviewing. What did they see, hear, feel, wonder?

It should be noted that shopping areas are not all bad. However, for Christians and non-Christians alike, they seem to capture the essence of the commercialism that has come to be associated with the Christmas season and often detract from the true spirit of this holy season, the season of preparing for Christmas and Christ's coming.

Sing a Christmas carol or two and then prepare to move on to the third and final part of the event.

The Event—Part 3

This part of the event is designed to help the participants put together the observations and learnings of the total event in a very real and tangible way as well as to provide some additional fun and festivity.

Four activity centers are suggested. These will need to have been prepared in advance in an area where you can spread out. Check the Bible references at the end of this article for use in centers #1 and #2. Depending on the size of the group, you may choose to do all four activity centers, dividing the total group into four small groups. Or with a smaller group you may want to choose to do one or two of the activities as a total group.

Activity Center #1

Create posters that capture the spirit of Advent. These may warn persons of the danger of the Christmas Crunch or give suggestions about styles of gift giving. Put these posters up around the church for the duration of Advent.

Activity Center #2

Create a commercial, skit, or pantomime that expresses the learning of this event. For example, participants may contrast the Christmas of the shopping mall with that of the church or focus on preserving the best and truest spirit of Christmas. Perhaps these "brief commercial announcements" could be done for an adult or younger Sunday church school class, in morning worship, or at some other all-church gathering.

Activity Center #3

Make symbolic gifts such as peace, hope, strength, or encouragement. How? Only your imagination limits you! Make plans to give these very real gifts away, perhaps to persons of special need within the congregation.

Activity Center #4

Make some actual gifts to be given to friends or family members. Perhaps people skilled in crafts could teach others to make candles, minibanners, decoupaged items, or other crafts. The best gifts are those that come from the hearts and hands of people dear to you.

How does one conclude such an event as this? With celebration, that's how! Share the products of the activity centers. Put up the posters; try out the commercials. Sing some more Christmas carols together or play some Christmas music. And for a finale, some sugar-coated, calorie-laden Christmas goodies seem to be in order!

Bible References on Giving

- Isaiah 9:6—The Messiah is given, a gift.
- Genesis 28:22—We give out of what God has given us.
- Matthew 10:8—Freely have you received; so you should freely give.
- John 14:27—Jesus gives as the world does not/cannot give.
- Acts 20:32–35—Happiness is in giving.
- Matthew 6:2–4—Give in secret; don't be "showy."
- Ephesians 2:8–10—Salvation is a gift.
- Mark 14:3–9—Jesus receives a gift.
- Matthew 2:1–12—The Magi brought gifts.

Sing a Joyful Christmas!

by Arline J. Ban

Listen . . . Do you hear what I hear? "Jingle Bells," "Rudolph the Red-Nosed Reindeer," and yes, a jazzed-up version of "Silent Night" are already blasting out of the speakers in the shopping mall. Why, the Thanksgiving holiday is not even here yet! Look . . . Do you see what I see? Christmas decorations are already in place. Their message is clear: Shop early! Buy your gifts while there is still a good selection. Television commercials are already at work. Clothed in the music of the season, they whet those unrealistic expectations of "getting gifts" in the imagination of our children. What happened to Advent? What happened to that time of anticipation, thanksgiving, joy, and yes, even the mystery of God's love? Indeed, those of us who work with children have a challenge to tell the story of the Good News in Christmas. One way is to let the message come through music.

Through the ages God's people have expressed their faith and feelings of thanksgiving and joy with song, dance, and the use of instruments. The Hebrews expressed their faith with psalms and chants.

> Sing to God all the world!
> Worship God with joy;
>   come before God with happy songs!
>   —Psalm 100:1–2, paraphrased

> Sing a new song to God,
> Praise God with dancing;
>   play drums and harps in praise of God.
>   —Psalm 149:1,3, paraphrased

The music of Christmas joy has its roots in Mary's Magnificat:

> "My heart praises the Lord;
>   my soul is glad because of God my
>   Savior . . ."
>   —Luke 1:46–47 (GNB)

And in the music that the shepherds heard, we have the song of praise to God:

> "Glory to God in the highest heaven,
>   and peace on earth to those with whom
>   he is pleased."
>   —Luke 2:14 (GNB)

Helping Children Praise Through Song

As God's people in this day and age we continue to sing our praises through song. We join in with the Christmas music; yet often the meaning can be lost with the pressures of our time. Our children also hear and sing the Christmas carols in various settings. The association of the Good News with the Christmas story is not always made, however.

The following suggestions are ways to help children tune their ears and senses to the message in the religious music of Christmas. Perhaps the Christmas story in music will create positive associations that will last through the growing years and shine through the bombardment of the secular holiday.

The following is a plan for a children's event to be held the first Sunday in Advent. The purpose of this special time is to guide children in an experience of Christmas music so that they may share in Advent with more meaning. In an informal setting, the children may:

- listen to the Christmas story in music;
- sing the Christmas carols together;
- experiment with various ways to respond to music.

Learning centers are suggested to give children a choice of activities. The activities are intended to help girls and boys to relax, express their feelings, and enjoy the religious music of Christmas that they can appreciate at their age level. Have you ever thought, *I only wish we had more time to work with creative activities? I wish we had more time to work with music?* If so, gather the children together and try this plan or one of the alternative suggestions.

Planning

- **When?** Set aside the first Sunday in Advent to gather the children together. You may choose the regularly scheduled church school time or another block of time (at least one hour).

- **Who?** Children in grades 1–6 can work well together in learning centers. However, in larger church schools, groupings of grades 1–3 and 4–6 might be a better arrangement.

  There is an advantage when regular church school teachers are involved. They are familiar with the girls and boys and usually are aware of their special interests and gifts. Other helpers could be adults or youth who understand the importance of enabling and encouraging children to express themselves. Special music ability need not be a qualification for a leader.

- **Where?** Use a room with enough space for gathering the group together comfortably. The room needs to lend itself to warmth and informality and be away from other groups that might be disturbed by the music.

- **Prepare.** Leaders will need to get together a few weeks ahead of time to work through the details of planning. Clarify your purpose. What do you hope to accomplish?

- **Decide.** Which learning centers will you use? Choose those that will appeal to your particular group of children. What other things can you do to make the experience more meaningful? For example, your congregation may be learning a new Christmas hymn for use during Advent. Check with your pastor or music director. Before deciding to use the music, check the words and music for their appropriateness with children.

Consider inviting persons from an ethnic group in your church or another congregation to share music from their tradition and culture.

How will you use space for learning centers? Is it possible to screen parts of a room with dividers, tables, or large boxes? Because of the variety of music and activities, consider using additional areas in other rooms.

Decide what materials and equipment will be needed for each center. Record players, Christmas records of good quality, tape recorders, and prerecorded tapes can be useful.

What charts need to be made ahead of time? Put the words of new songs to be learned on large charts. Make charts that outline the steps to follow, and post these instructions in each center.

What Christmas pictures and posters can you hang on the walls of the room to make it more attractive?

In your planning keep in mind that large numbers of persons are not required for learning centers. If no more than two or three children choose a center, they can have a meaningful time.

Gathering the Children

Let Christmas music fill the air as the children gather. If you know someone who plays the Autoharp or guitar well, enlist the person (or persons) to accompany the music in these opening moments.

Ask the children, "What did you see or what did you hear in the past few days that tells you Christmas is coming? How do you feel when you think about Christmas?"

Explain that this Sunday is the first Sunday in Advent. Talk about Advent as a time of waiting and getting ready for Christmas. Younger children will understand that it is a time of being excited, happy, and thankful that Jesus was born. Older children may understand Advent as the time of waiting that is symbolic of the Hebrews' wait for the fulfillment of the promise of the Messiah.

Call attention to the special ways your church anticipates Christmas or celebrates Advent. Some of your traditions might be the Advent wreath, the Christmas crèche, or the decorations put up in the church by families. Help to prepare the children for what they might expect in church events and worship.

Sing one or two familiar carols and refer to the biblical story told in them.

Call attention to the learning centers. Describe what might happen in each center. Encourage the children to choose which activities they would like to do.

Learning Centers

Moving Creatively to a Familiar Carol

Children usually have vivid imaginations. Using

those imaginations and their sense of rhythm and movement, children can act out the words of the carol with creative movements. The girls and boys can do simple movements to "Go Tell It on the Mountain," a black spiritual.

Listen to the carol and then sing it together. Talk about the story it tells and the feelings expressed in the words. The following example is just one way to combine music with physical movement. Do use the ideas of the children. Ask, "How could we move our bodies to dramatize these verses?"

1. Go tell it on the mountain
   (*Lift feet as if climbing a mountain.*)

2. Over the hills and everywhere
   (*Stretch arms out in front and move them slowly apart to join hands with others in circle.*)

3. Go, tell it on the mountain
   (*Lift feet as if climbing a mountain.*)

4. That Jesus Christ is born
   (*Walk to the left with hands cupped to the mouth as if shouting, and then move to the right.*)

Other phrases to substitute for lines 1 and 3 might be the following:
Go, tell about the shepherds . . .
Go, tell about the manger . . .
Go, tell about the baby . . .

Learning a New Carol

There is a wide selection of Christmas carols based on the biblical story. Choose one that is not familiar to the children. Be sure it has some pep or rhythm that children will respond to readily. The words and music need to be quickly understood without too much explanation. Here are suggestions:

- "Go, Tell It on the Mountain"—a black spiritual
- "Mary Had a Baby, Yes, God"—a traditional American carol
- " 'Twas in the Moon of Wintertime"—a carol of the Huron Indian people
- "Hey! Hey! Anybody Listening"—a contemporary carol by Richard Avery and Donald Marsh

Two songbooks to use as resources for these and other carols are: *Ready, Set . . . Sing!* (Valley Forge: Judson Press, available September 1989), $8.95; *Sing to God: Songs and Hymns for Christian Education* (New York: United Church Press, 1984), $9.95.

In a comfortable setting, perhaps sitting informally on a rug, listen first to the music. A good recording might be used, accompanied by an Autoharp or guitar. Say the words of the carol together. Discuss these questions: What is the story it tells? What is the main concept in the carol? Listen to the music again. This time encourage the children to hum, snap fingers, clap hands, or tap feet. Then sing it together just for enjoyment, not for perfection. In any additional time, the children might enjoy pantomiming what phrases mean.

Making a Joyful Noise with Rhythm Instruments

Children can have fun making their own instruments from all sorts of material and even "junk." Collect things that have a potential for musical noise. Here are some suggestions for this activity:

- Clap dowels together.
- Wrap sandpaper around blocks of wood. When blocks are scraped together, they make a delightful noise.
- Aluminum pie pans can be taped together with small stones or old beads inside to make shakers.
- Bells of any size can be played singly or strung together for effect.
- Tongue depressors moving across metal cake racks make an interesting sound.
- Cardboard tubes can act as trumpets.
- Empty coffee cans or cardboard containers (like oatmeal boxes) make good drums.

Choose familiar Christmas music that has real pep and a beat to it with possibilities for accompaniment. Play the music through while the children listen. Use a piano, guitar, Autoharp, commercial recordings, or music that you have pretaped especially for this event. After listening, discuss what story the carol tells. Ask the children to listen again and to imagine what kinds of instruments might fit the music. What do they hear as they listen? Talk over the possibilities. List them. Then look over the collected materials to decide what could be made into an instrument and who will do it. When the instruments are finished, play them all together with the music. As time permits, go over the music several times, assigning different parts to the various instruments.

Creating a Musical Ensemble

If there are boys and girls in your church who play musical instruments such as flute, violin, or trumpet, invite them ahead of time to bring their instruments for this event. (Your music director may need to help provide music in the proper key for each instrument.) They can form their own interest group to play just for fun or plan to play together for another occasion in the church.

Singing with the Organ

Make arrangements with the organist of your church to work with a small group of children during this event. This would be an opportunity for them to get close to the organ, touch it, and listen to it. The organist might explain how the organ works and demonstrate for them how various instrumental sounds can be created by the organ. At this time the children might listen to one or two of the Christmas selections that will be used in the worship services during Advent. Singing favorite carols along with the organ could also make this a special time for children.

Responding to Music with Illustrating

Plan a center for those children who prefer to draw. While listening to Christmas music, they may choose from a variety of materials to express their feelings or ideas, to make a design, or to create a picture that tells the Christmas story. Some children may enjoy finger painting designs to express their feelings. Others may create a picture or express feelings or ideas with some of the following materials: colored chalk, colored felt-tip pens, crayons, paints, bits of cloth, or various shapes of colored paper. Try to provide more than one kind of background paper, including newsprint, butcher paper, and brown bags.

Provide plenty of old newspapers to protect floor or table space where the children work. Choose recordings of the traditional carols that tell the story of Christmas (for example: "Silent Night," "Away in a Manger," "We Three Kings"). Listen to a portion of the music and then stop and ask the children to identify the part of the Christmas story to which the music refers. Repeat this with another recording, playing only a part of the music. Then ask the children to tell the whole Christmas story.

Acquaint the children with the choices of materials they have, and explain that they are free to express their feelings and ideas while listening. Ask these questions: What does the music say to them? What kind of movement—slow, fast, rhythmic—does it suggest? How could they put this on paper?

The emphasis will be on enjoying the activity and the freedom to express themselves without having expectations of a finished product or a work of art to show.

Celebrating Together

Allow enough time for the children to come together for the closing moments. Encourage them to share what they did in the learning centers. What did they enjoy? What would they like to do again? What new things did they learn? Close with a prayer and the singing of a new or familiar carol.

Thinking It Over

You will note that there is no emphasis on children performing for others in these suggestions. The focus is on experiencing music so as to enrich the meaning of Christmas for the girls and boys. However, out of these experiences may grow an idea of sharing Christmas music with the shut-ins of your congregation or community.

Variations

A Christmas card workshop for children could be held on a Saturday or Sunday afternoon. Precede it with a game period. Extend the time for activities. Use some of the illustrations made by the children during the event to decorate the halls of the church. Plan to have the children contribute to corporate worship with the movement to music that they created. Close with a sharing time and special treats.

This plan could be used as a basis for a family/intergenerational event. Begin with a fun-and-games time to help people relax and get to know one another better. Enjoy a shared meal together. Include an opportunity for families and singles to get together in small groups and share their stories about favorite Christmas memories, favorite carols, and particular family Christmas traditions.

Write Your Own Advent Devotional Booklet

by Joseph H. Gaunt

The latent spark of communicative creativity that's smoldering among members of your congregation may be kindled into flame through the inspiration of a unique project that taps a variety of talents—the publication of a booklet of Advent devotional readings. Writers from your church will enjoy putting their Christmastide reveries and reminiscences onto paper, while other members can exercise their editing talents to blend the copy submitted into a unified and inspiring publication. After additional contributors have invested their typing abilities and still others have collated and stapled the booklets, the most satisfying opportunity for involvement takes place as copies are distributed to everyone in the congregational family and the church neighborhood.

Those are the special advantages discovered during preparation of an Advent devotional booklet by the First Baptist Church of Green Bay, Wisconsin, under the leadership of its pastor. Those who helped to develop the Yuletide publication enthusiastically recommend it to your congregation as both an inspirational guide to Christmas and an evangelistic tool for neighborhood distribution.

Writers of the meditations brought to their devotionals such diverse backgrounds as that of a ninety-four-year-old widow who is a shut-in at a nursing home, a production artist for an advertising firm, a retired high school social studies teacher, and the news service director and a television production specialist from the University of Wisconsin.

From the wealth of their experience these writers contributed thoughts on such domestic topics as decorating Christmas cookies; appropriate gifts for children; family and church Christmas Eve worship services; how memories are created; sharing time with loved ones; the evolution of a family circle through the generations; gifts of one's self drawn from personal resources in lieu of expensive, inflation-ridden presents; an address book whose pages chronicle forgotten friendships; the value of a gift from a friend; as well as a poem of twelve couplets lamenting the Christmas rush.

Other devotional readings centered on the church memories of a Christmas Eve service conducted in 1910, a reprise of the past summer's most challenging sermon with a call to evaluate the effects of putting its principles into practice, and a thirty-six-line poem paraphrasing Luke's Christmas story. From the world of work came meditations describing a schoolroom bulletin board decorated for the holidays and the plight of a radio announcer working alone on Christmas Day. One compelling devotional drawn from the world at large juxtaposed the Christmas story with typical headlines printed in a daily newspaper.

These readings were grouped in four sections, arranged by the weeks of Advent: the season's first period, a time of anticipation; the second week, preparation; third week of Advent, memories; and the fourth period, a time to experience.

A recommended production schedule to guide your congregation through the project of publishing an Advent devotional booklet calls for drafting manuscripts during the months of September and October, followed by editing, typing, and printing during November. Distribute the booklets to the congregation on the Sunday after Thanksgiving and encourage each member to take additional copies as gifts to neighbors and schoolmates, as well as to colleagues at the office and workplace. When your church distributes copies of the booklet to homes on all the streets near its building, follow up the distribution effort with an invitation to Sunday church school, worship services, and special holiday activities.

The project need not become expensive. The mechanics of printing the booklet by the Green Bay congregation involved typing the meditations at the church office, followed by offset printing of four pages on the front and back of each legal-size sheet. Each booklet comprised seven such sheets of paper. Its cover design consisted of artwork symbolic of the season, followed by an opening page written by the pastor. The back cover remained blank for a personal note to a friend who might receive the copy by mail or directly from a member.

The effort of collating and mailing provides another opportunity for fellowship and activity. Arranging transportation to the church for the elderly but active members would allow them to participate in this stage of production. Send them home with extra copies for friends they meet in senior citizens' activities and in their neighborhoods, as well as for service people such as newspaper carriers, mail carriers, and tradespersons with whom they have contact.

The Advent devotional booklet your church publishes can be distributed with pride as locally developed material with specific references that are uniquely appropriate to your area, to nearby residents, and to the season as celebrated among your congregation and in your region.

Make a Progressive Banner for Advent and Christmas

by Mary Nelson Keithahn

In recent years churches of many denominations have begun the practice of hanging special banners in their sanctuaries during Advent and Christmas. Our church also has chosen to celebrate the beginning of the Christian year in this way. The banners that have hung in our sanctuary have been somewhat unique in two ways: (1) They have been "progressive," and (2) they have correlated with the Sunday services of worship and other areas of church life.

Progressive banners are appropriate for the season of Advent, since it is a time of waiting and preparation for the coming of Christ. A progressive banner is one designed to be hung in an unfinished state; different parts of the design are added at regular intervals (for example, each Sunday during Advent) so that it is completed by a specific time (Christmas Eve or Christmas Day). The theme of our first banner was the Nativity story from Luke 2:1–20. Figures and key words from the story were added weekly during Advent. On Christmas Eve the banner was completed, providing an illustration of the newborn Jesus and the adoration of the shepherds. Our second banner told the Nativity story from Matthew 2:1–11 in the same way. Both banners served the dual purpose of marking off the weeks of waiting during Advent and telling the story of Christ's birth.[1]

With careful joint planning by those responsible for worship, music, and education in the church, the themes of our progressive banners have been correlated with the Sunday services of worship and other areas of church life. Since the banners are hung in the sanctuary, they have provided the focal point for the Scripture, sermon texts, hymns, and anthems in each service of worship. The themes of the banners grew out of the sermon texts selected by the minister. Related hymns and anthems were chosen with the help of the organist and choir directors. In addition, resources based on the themes of the banners were developed for family worship at home (for example, Advent calendars or Advent wreaths with worship guides). These were distributed to church families. The annual Sunday church school programs also were related to the banner themes.

The theme of our most recent progressive banner for Advent and Christmas was the "Prologue to John's Gospel" (John 1:1–18). In this passage the writer expresses the belief that in Jesus God has fulfilled the promises made to the people of Israel from the time of creation down through the centuries, and that promise has been extended to all believers everywhere. We decided that the symbol of the "Jesse Tree" would provide a good medium for recalling God's promises that were fulfilled in Jesus.

The Jesse Tree is a Christian art form based on the imagery in Isaiah 11:1–2, and it dates back to medieval times. The early form of the tree showed Jesse, father of King David, in a reclining position. From him springs a tree or vine bearing David and showing Jesus at the very top. A later form of the Jesse Tree had other figures from the Old Testament added. The Jesse Tree thus became a sort of family tree for Jesus, showing his ancestors, both spiritual and biological. All of these characters had received God's promises that were fulfilled in Jesus.

With this design in mind, the following outline was prepared for the services of worship on the Advent Sundays and Christmas Eve.[2]

---

[1] We have always glued the banner pieces onto the backing when the banner was completed, and we have used it as a regular banner in succeeding years. Others have used pins or Velcro fasteners to attach the pieces temporarily so that the banners could be reused as progressive banners.

[2] The board of Christian education also designed and prepared Jesse Tree Advent calendars, and the annual Sunday church school pageant was planned around the theme of promise and fulfillment.

First Sunday in Advent

Texts: Genesis 1:1—2:4; John 1:1–18 (especially 1:1–5)
Hymns: "We Praise Thee, O God"; "Praise to the Living God"; "Come, Ye Thankful People, Come"
Key Word: MAKE
Sermon Title: "The Word of God Creates"

(The gift of life from God is not completed in creation. Rather, it is a continuing act fulfilled in the gift of new life in Christ through his Spirit.)

Banner Figures: Jesse Tree with Jesse in reclining position at its base.

Second Sunday in Advent

Texts: Genesis 17:1–21; John 1:16; Hebrews 12:1–24
Hymns: "O My Soul, Bless God the Father"; "Praise the Lord! Ye Heavens Adore Him"; "O Little Town of Bethlehem"
Key Word: CALL
Sermon Title: "God's Call and Our Response"

(God's call to us was initiated through Abraham and Sarah, and it was fulfilled in Jesus.)

Banner Figures: Abraham and Sarah

Third Sunday in Advent

Texts: Deuteronomy 10:1–22; John 1:1–17 (especially 1:17)
Hymns: "The God of Abraham Praise"; "O Come, O Come, Emmanuel"; "Come, Thou Long-Expected Jesus"
Key Word: RULE
Sermon Title: "The King Rules"

(The kingdom of God that was moved forward by the giving of the law of Moses and the establishment of a holy nation under David was fulfilled in Jesus' proclamation of God's rule and invitation to accept it.)

Banner Figures: Moses and David

Fourth Sunday in Advent

Texts: Isaiah 11:1–9; Luke 1:26–38; John 1:6–9
Hymns: "On Jordan's Banks the Baptist's Cry"; "Comfort, Comfort Now My People"; "Hail to the Lord's Anointed"
Key Word: TELL
Sermon Title: "I Have Good News and Bad News"

(The bad news is that God's response to our selfish ways is "No!" The good news is that God's "Yes!" comes to all who receive Jesus.)

Banner Figures: Isaiah and Mary

Christmas Eve

Text: John 1:14[3]
Hymns: "O Come, All Ye Faithful"; "Let All Mortal Flesh Keep Silence"; "Silent Night"
Key Word: LIVE
Sermon Title: "Live"

(The "good life" is not an idea or a principle, but it is what results when we let the spirit of Christ live in us. This is the real fulfillment of God's promises.)

Banner Figure: Jesus

In constructing the banner, the committee members followed these steps: (1) Use 2½ yards of 36-inch-wide burlap in old gold for the backing. (2) Machine-stitch a 2½-inch-wide casing at the top for a rod. (3) Across the bottom of the banner iron on a strip of woven interfacing. (4) Cut the bottom of the banner into five triangular-shaped tabs, each measuring 8 inches from tip to center base and 7 1/5 inches across at the widest point. (5) At the bottom of each tab sew 5-inch tassels made from gold yarn. (6) Across the banner, just above the tabs, glue a strip of ½-inch flat gold braid.

All of the letters for the banner were cut from white felt and glued in place as indicated. In addition to the key words for the tabs, the committee felt it would be helpful to add the names of the figures.

The trunk of the Jesse Tree was cut from brown burlap and backed with iron-on woven interfacing.[4] We used a pattern made by enlarging and elongating the cover illustration from a book, *The Jesse Tree.*[5] The tree was outlined with brown yarn. The leaves were olive green burlap, outlined with green yarn.

Banner committee members worked on the figures individually so that they would be completed and ready to glue into place when needed. They used an overhead projector to enlarge the figure patterns which they found in several different resources.[6] All of the figures were made from

---

[3]The Scripture was interpreted by church youth as they pantomimed the story "Peter and the Hermit," adapted from the Cathedral filmstrip (1963) of that title.

[4]Committee members have found that such interfacing makes burlap easier to handle and prevents it from raveling before it is glued into place.

[5]*The Jesse Tree,* by Raymond and Georgene Anderson (Minneapolis: Augsburg Fortress Publishers, 1966).

[6]Patterns for Jesse, David, Mary, Moses, and Isaiah were taken from *Wait in Joyful Hope!* by Mary V. Reilly, Margaret K. Wetterer, and Nancy K. Lyons (Wilton, Conn.: Morehouse-Barlow Co. Inc., 1980), pp.10–11. $3.95.

felt, with accents provided by marking pens, yarn, sequins, and braid. Details for each figure were as follows:

Jesse—gray and brown robe, outlined in gray yarn; absorbent-cotton hair and beard.

Abraham—blue tunic with lavender aba and skullcap, outlined in dark lavender yarn; white absorbent-cotton beard and hair; brown yarn belt; brown burlap staff.

Sarah—pink tunic, outlined in pink yarn; lavender overdrape, outlined in blue; blue headpiece; gold yarn earring.

Moses—light blue tunic with dark blue sleeve, outlined in medium blue yarn; gray felt tablets, outlined in gray yarn, with numerals added by black marking pen.

David—cerise robe, outlined in light pink yarn with white sleeve lining; brown felt hair and beard with brown yarn overlay; shiny gold fabric crown and harp; star sequins on crown; gold cord strings on lyre.

Isaiah—navy blue tunic, outlined in gray yarn; gray scroll with black writing; brown felt beard and hair, black sandals.

Mary—light blue gown, outlined with medium blue yarn; white headpiece, outlined in white yarn; brown hair, brown felt shoes, outlined in blue yarn.

Jesus—white tunic and aba, outlined with purple yarn; purple sleeve lining; white headpiece, outlined in pink; black felt sandals; brown felt hair.

Like our other progressive banners made in years past, this Jesse Tree banner helped our church members of all ages to wait with faith and understanding for the promises of Advent to be fulfilled again on Christ's birthday. We encourage others to design and make a progressive banner for Advent and Christmas.

NOTE: Patterns for Abraham, Sarah, and Jesus were adapted from figures from flannelgraph sets called ''Pict-o-Graph Series,'' published by Standard Publishing Company, Cincinnati, Ohio.

Christmas Outdoors

1. A Live Outdoor Nativity Scene

How could a church be united in a single project that would involve a great number of people, a great amount of talent, and have an impact on more than just that particular church? A huge order! But there was a way, a way that worked—a LIVE NATIVITY SCENE!

One of the positive sides to a project like this was the many skills it demanded. People were needed in the following areas: carpentry, sewing, makeup, audiovisual, verbal, administrative, and refreshment. Also needed were people who were willing to stand as characters in the scene.

After we decided to schedule the event for the five evenings preceding Christmas, a most important starting point was to find two coordinators who work well together to oversee the project.

Through bulletin inserts and the church newsletter the members of the congregation were given the opportunity to select on which of the following committees they wished to serve. After this information was gathered, the committees were formed, with a chairperson for each.

The BUILDING COMMITTEE drew up the plan and built the stable.

Since we used two alternating sets of characters each evening, the COSTUME COMMITTEE made two complete sets of costumes. Each alternating scene was composed of two angels, Mary, Joseph, three wise men, and three shepherds, making a total of twenty characters needed for each evening. The women used their ingenuity to create the costumes. At least one small shepherd boy was part of the scene, too.

The MAKEUP AND DRESSING COMMITTEE was in charge of making the beards. The material was purchased from a theatrical supply house. The same beards were used all five evenings. The committee also was responsible each evening for putting the makeup and beards on the characters.

The MUSIC AND WORD COMMITTEE made two two-hour tapes to be used as background music. This committee also set up outdoor speakers which we were able to borrow from our community. These tapes consisted of Christmas music, with Scripture reading interspersed throughout. By having two-hour tapes, there was no need to switch tapes during the evening, and we could alternate the tapes each night.

The LIGHTING AND ACOUSTICS COMMITTEE put the spotlights in position and saw to it that the wiring was in place each evening.

The ANIMALS COMMITTEE borrowed two sheep and a donkey and found lodging for them near the church. Each evening this committee was responsible for taking the animals to and from the scene.

The CHARACTER COORDINATING COMMITTEE had a big job. This committee had to assign twenty people an evening to be characters as well as have others serve as backup in case someone could not make it. For three consecutive Sundays, a schedule was handed out in church asking people to sign up for a particular evening on which they could participate.

The KITCHEN COMMITTEE had a chairperson for each evening of the scene who saw to it that coffee, hot chocolate, and cookies were provided for the various committee members, the participants, and those members and friends of the congregation who wished to stop by for a moment of fellowship.

This Christmas project involved over 120 people. The cost was around five hundred dollars, obtained from designated gifts. The scene was enacted for five evenings, two hours each evening. We found that the cast could stand comfortably for only twenty minutes at a time; so we had several shifts for each group. We were interested in having it at the busiest shopping time; so early evening (7:00–9:00 P.M.) seemed most appropriate. Because of the shelter the building provided, the weather did not hinder us on any evening.

Many people remarked that, being in the downtown area, the Nativity scene was a constant reminder of what Christmas is all about. For us as a church, it presented a worthwhile challenge and made us feel we had made a contribution to the entire community.

One of the effects was that the scene caused a stillness in the crowd that gathered. Some who came stopped, and tears rolled down their cheeks; children's eyes widened as they realized the animals were real; many just stood and looked.

Night after night they came to see the simple gospel story portrayed in this way.

—*Frederick W. Young*

2. Christmas in the Barn

Christmas in the Barn? That idea fascinated me. I had come to Ottumwa, Iowa, from New York State, and I had never heard of anything like *Christmas in the Barn.* I was a little skeptical at first, but I found the program delightful.

We arrived at the barn at about four o'clock in the afternoon. The cows were displaced for a while by our presence. Because it was cold and rainy, they stood impatiently at the gate waiting for us to vacate their accommodations. Their presence added a realistic quality to the proceedings. A moo now and then during the program was a great, natural mood setter. Cats moved freely about the barn while the program went on. Two horses were in an enclosed area where we could see them. They seemed to listen to the entire program. Last year, I'm told, when one of them stuck its nose over the boards, a child shouted, "Look! There's a camel!" The narration was interspersed with meows, a few moos, and several well-placed neighs.

What do you do at *Christmas in the Barn?* The audience sat on bales of hay. A husband and wife team narrated the Christmas story, and the choir director led us in singing familiar Christmas songs. Both adults and children were called out of the audience to be shepherds, wise men (and women), and angels. A baby became baby Jesus. The hay in the manger added reality to the scene. We even had the smells of Christmas!

—*David Bevington*

3. A Christmas Hayride

Would you like to do something different for a Christmas caroling activity? Try a Christmas hayride. Whether you belong to a big city church or a country church, this can be an event of fun, enjoyment, and spiritual growth. Before making plans for a hayride, check to see that your church's liability insurance will cover the activity, that local government ordinances allow such an activity, and that your vehicle is properly equipped and licensed for the road.

Results? A collection of people of all ages share a heartwarming experience together. New bonds are established among people who may not come together in other activities. The Good News of Christ is shared with others as voices blend in joyful noels.

—*Jane Landreth*

Gifts to Make

Ideas shared by Rebecca Dobson, Virginia Rich, Ruth Spencer, and Anne N. Rupp

What is Advent all about but getting ready for Christmas? What is Christmas all about but celebrating the gift of God's Son to the world? The Advent season of preparation can be filled with the joy of making gifts for others as a celebration of Christmas.

The suggestions that follow may be made in workshops, in church school classes, or in homes by children, youth, adults, or by intergenerational groups.

Ornaments

Ornaments make nice gifts to put on a Christmas tree or to hang in a window or on a wall. Do some research about Christmas symbols. In addition to the traditional symbols of Christmas, add symbols that stand for meaningful things connected with your own congregation. Perhaps your church has strong ties with a mission program in another country; you could choose a symbol to represent that country. Local church projects could also be included.

One way to make the tree ornaments is to cut them from Styrofoam, which could be collected by saving meat trays from the supermarket. A uniform and pleasing effect can be made by using only the white trays. First make paper patterns of the symbols you have chosen. In all of these projects it is wise to keep the designs very simple and stylized. Place the pattern on the Styrofoam and draw around it. Then cut out the ornament, using a pocket or paring knife.

Another way to make beautiful, uniform ornaments is to decorate white eggs with the symbols you want to depict. You must first blow out the contents of the raw egg. Make a hole in both ends of the egg, using a thick yarn needle or a thin nail. Be sure to pierce the yolk of the egg with the needle or nail. Blow into one hole, and the egg will be forced out of the other one. Rinse the eggshell and let it drain and dry. To put the symbol on the egg, use watercolor paint or felt-tip pens. If you hesitate to draw directly onto the egg, do the drawing on tracing or tissue paper and then glue the design onto the egg with white glue. Glue a loop of thread to the top of the egg to serve as a hanger.

To make cloth ornaments, use an old sheet or buy some unbleached muslin. Cut two circles for each ornament. It is best to make them all the same size. Sew two pieces together, leaving a small opening. Turn each inside out, fill with pillow stuffing, and sew up the opening. An alternative way is to sew the pieces together, leaving half the circle unstitched. Turn inside out and insert a circle of cardboard. Finish off by turning in the remaining edges and hand-stitching.

Designs can be put onto the cloth in several ways. You can paint the designs with artist's acrylic paint (which comes in tubes) or use thickly applied crayon. If you plan to use crayon on the soft stuffed circles, you should add the design before stuffing the ornament. Embroidery is the most time-consuming way of decorating these cloth ornaments, but it gives a beautiful effect.

An attractive ornament can be made from a rubber canning-jar ring. Cut off the tab and cover the ring with yarn, using the blanket stitch. This will be easier if the yarn (about 10 feet) is wound in a small ball first and unwound as needed. When the ring is completely covered, make a loop for hanging. Add a perky bow, hang a small bell in the center, or glue on holly leaves and berries of green and red felt. To make a lapel ornament, tape a small safety pin to the ring before covering it with yarn.

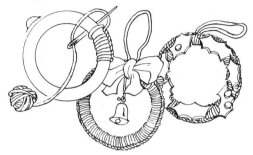

Photos

Persons who can't get out to church would enjoy the gift of a set of pictures of the decorated church, events, and people.

Bed or Chair Pocket

One yard of 45-inch fabric will make three pockets. Cut the cloth from side to side so that you get three pieces 12 inches by 45 inches. Turn under ½ inch at both ends and sew. Then turn up one end 9 inches with the hem folded to the outside. Stitch along the 9-inch sides ½ inch from the edges. Turn this part inside out so that the seams are on the inside. Then turn under both of the long sides ½ inch and sew those edges, making sure the hem is on the side away from the pocket. The long strip can then be put under the mattress of a bed with the pocket hanging down. It can also be put under the cushion of a chair with the pocket extending up over the arm of the chair, thus providing a place to keep things within reach.

Note Holder

1. Use two paper plates; cut one in half.
2. Punch holes in the plates.

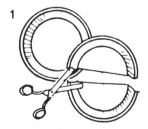

3. Sew them together with string, ribbon, or yarn as shown in the illustration.
4. Add a string at the top for hanging.

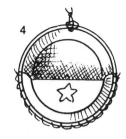

A Christmas Mobile

1. Cut a paper plate in spiral shape.
2. Punch holes in the paper plate.
3. Hang decorations on the mobile with string or yarn. The decorations can be made from colored paper.

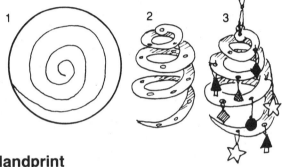

Handprint

1. On a paper plate draw around one hand or dip the palm of one hand in finger paint and press on the plate.
2. Punch a hole in the top and attach a loop of string for hanging.

Flannel Board (For a Church School Class)

Use felt or flannel to cover a piece of plywood or other sturdy material such as tri-wall cardboard. Wrap it around the edges and staple or tape it with cloth tape on the back.

Figures or shapes to be used on the flannel board can be made of Pellon, felt, or sturdy paper. Pellon is a type of nonwoven lining material sold at fabric stores. It can be drawn on with felt-tip pens or crayons. It is available in several weights; the heavy weight is best for this use. Both Pellon and felt will stick to the flannel board as they are. Paper figures must have small pieces of sandpaper, felt, or flannel glued to the back of them. Story pieces, shapes, numbers, and letters are all useful with a flannel board.

Stencils

Collect the plastic tops of margarine tubs, coffee cans, and the like. Draw simple outline shapes and objects on the lids with a felt-tip marker. Cut the shapes out carefully with small sharp scissors. The stencils are now ready to be used over and over by children with their crayons.

Pin Cushion

Cut a circle from a gallon plastic jug, or use the plastic top from a coffee can or margarine container. Cut a larger circle from cloth. Fill it with pillow stuffing or nylon stockings. Tie or tape it into a ball and glue it to the plastic circle.

A Living Wreath

Root some slips of philodendron or fast-growing ivy. Plant them in containers that have been decorated. Cans or large plastic containers work well. Before planting, punch holes in the bottom of the containers for drainage. Place each potted plant on a coaster, a large lid decorated to match the pot. Make the wreath form from a wire hanger with two prongs placed in the soil. Cover the curved wire with green yarn or floral tape. The plant can be trained around the wire to form a living wreath. Fasten a red bow or other decoration at the top. When the gift is ready to be delivered, put it in a decorated grocery bag, fold the top once, and staple shut.

A Mini-box

You will think of many uses for a mini-box. To make the top of the box: (1) Cut an exact square, 5 inches on each side, from a colorful picture, greeting card, calendar, church bulletin, or magazine. (2) On the back (which need not be plain) draw light pencil lines between opposite corners that will cross in the center. (3) Fold each corner to the center; crease well. (4) Leaving the points folded in, fold opposite *sides* (not corners) to the center; crease well. Unfold and repeat with the other two sides. (5) Open to the position in step 3. Cut four slits, two each on opposite sides. Cut on the vertical fold line, from the edge to the first horizontal fold. (6) Unfold and cut off the 4 smallest triangles that are formed. (7) Unfold the two sides between the slits. Form box sides by bending up the outside edges of the remaining sides and by folding in wings to form the alternate sides. (8) Secure wings by lifting the opened points over them, folding them in the inside so that the points are at the center of the box lid.

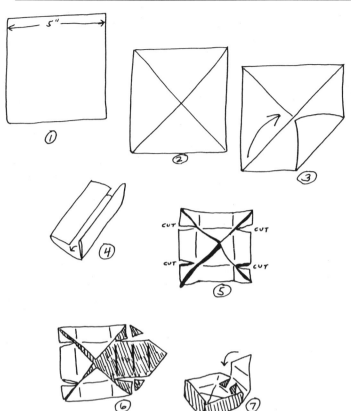

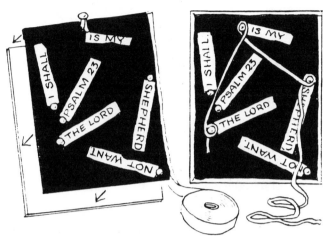

The box bottom is made the same way, beginning with a square ¼ inch shorter on each side. For younger children do not use heavy paper. Encourage thoughtful selection of the cover picture to match the interests of the recipient. A box may contain a message of love, a poem, or coupons for services that the child will perform either at a specified time or as requested. Make nests of boxes, beginning with squares of 4, 5, and 6 inches. A colorful box makes an attractive tree decoration.

A Puzzle

A puzzle is a good gift for all ages. To make "Quick Quotes," select a Bible verse and print it carefully on a narrow strip of paper. Cut the strip into phrases. Glue these phrases at random on a piece of cardboard about 8½ by 11 inches. At the right end of each phrase, insert a paper fastener through the cardboard, spread the ends on the back, and cover them with masking tape. Cover the entire back of the puzzle with a second piece of cardboard. Tape the edges together. Tie a piece of yarn to the fastener beside the first phrase of the verse. To do the puzzle, loop the yarn around

Jewelry/Ring Holder

Bend coat hanger wire into the shape of a child's hand. Insert the ends in a 3-by-6-inch board or in a container of plaster of Paris.

Napkin Ring

Cut a 1½-inch section from a cardboard tube. Decorate it with fabric, lace, artificial flowers, or felt.

Pot Holder

There are many different kinds of crayons and markers that work well on fabric. You may want to take a piece of the cloth you plan to use for the potholders to a craft store to experiment before selecting the most suitable instrument. It is a good idea to draw your design on paper first. When it looks the way you want it, draw it on the fabric, following the instructions provided with the crayons or markers. Sew a back and front together, leaving a space to fill the holder.

Candles

Candles are gifts suggesting light and cheer. Several short candles floating in a bowl of water surrounded by greens form a lovely centerpiece. To prepare, place old candles or paraffin in a can. Set the can in a pot of water on the stove and heat carefully. Remember, wax is flammable! Add wax crayon chips for color. Remove unused wicks from melted wax and stretch out on newspaper to dry. Fill small gelatin molds or paper or plastic cups with melted wax about 1½ inches deep. As the wax cools, insert a 2-inch piece of wick. Remove from molds when thoroughly hardened.

To make a cracked-ice candle, melt wax or paraffin, colored if you wish. Remove top from milk or juice carton (pint, quart, or half-gallon size) and rinse. Crack ice cubes in large and medium pieces, drain water, and return to freezer. Select a center candle as tall as the carton (a good use for cracked, misshapen, or discolored candles). Pour ½ inch of melted wax in bottom of carton. Center candle in the carton and surround it loosely with cracked ice. Pour remaining hot wax over the ice. When thoroughly hardened, remove carton, allowing water to drain. Add ribbon, foil, or greenery for decoration.

Stained Glass Windows

Paul Schrock

A stained glass effect can be used to decorate your church (or home) for the Advent season. Discuss ideas and decide what you want to express on glass. You may want to create one picture to which each person contributes a part, or you may want to make a series of motifs or symbols or pictures.

How do you make a stained glass picture? Cut newsprint the size of your window. Now draw the scenes or story you wish to portray. Tape the paper to the outside of the window with the sketched picture facing you. Now you are ready to paint on the window. You may choose to paint various parts of the scene with tempera paint. You will want to do some experimenting with the tempera paint. Some types or colors crack or run more easily than others. For a "leaded" effect on your "stained glass" window, use a broad black felt-tip pen.

You may want to work out a lighting effect so that passersby may see your scene after dusk.

Another Way

1. Cut shapes in *two* pieces of construction paper, in the same place.

2. Apply paste on top of bottom sheet.
3. Cover holes on bottom sheet with pieces of tissue paper of different colors.

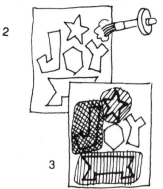

4. Turn top sheet over and apply paste.
5. Paste the two sheets of paper together.
6. Hang the finished picture in a window so the light will shine through it.

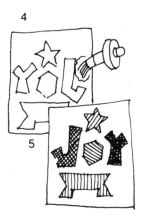

Write an Advent Hymn— And Share It

by Barbara C. Blossom

Advent is a fitting time to study the prophecies foretelling the Messiah's coming. Getting students interested in this subject is a challenge for most teachers.

One method you may wish to consider is hymn writing. It is an activity that can be done by children, youth, and adults, or by an intergenerational group. Here's how!

Background

A good starting point for a study of the prophecies is a look at what Palestine was like for the Jews in the years preceding the birth of Jesus. Roman officials governed their lives. Dishonest tax collectors extorted as much money as they could from even the poorest people. Families were split apart at slave auctions, some being sold to one country, some to another. Life was generally hard and unpleasant.

It had been that way for a long time. Before the Romans, other countries had conquered the Jews. The people didn't know how long they could go on, but they had hope. Many years before, prophets had spoken of a Messiah coming to save them. They had faith that God would not forget them. Through the years they repeated over and over the words of the prophets telling of God's promise to send a Savior. They prayed that their Savior would come soon.

Suggest an Advent Hymn

With this background, you can move easily to the prophecies. After the prophecies are read and discussed by your class, suggest that the students write an Advent hymn based on their studies.

The class that I teach wrote an Advent hymn and later shared it at a Sunday service. I didn't mention the possibility of presenting it in church when we started; it's better to see what develops.

Procedure

1. Study the background material (see above).
2. Read and talk about the following prophecies: Isaiah 2:4; Isaiah 11:6; Micah 5:2–3; Isaiah 11:1–3; Isaiah 7:14; Isaiah 9:6–7; Isaiah 60:1–3; Jeremiah 23:5; Isaiah 53:3–7.
3. Assign a prophecy to each student or to groups of two or three. Persons who might hesitate to try on their own might be able to work more easily with a group. If it is not possible to work with all the prophecies suggested, choose from the list the ones you wish to use.
4. Choose a simple hymn tune with an even rhythm. "Tallis' Canon" (one of the tunes we use for the Doxology) works well. It's familiar to most and easily learned for the rest. "Old Hundredth" works well also.
5. Sing or say the hymn together as you and the children beat out the rhythm. For example: "Praise God from whom all blessings flow. . . ." Do this several times until you're sure everyone has the beat.
6. Write an introductory first verse to help the students get the idea. This one will work, or you can write your own.

> The prophets spoke so long ago
> About a Savior who would show
> The Jews that God was still their God.
> And God would send a "mighty rod."

Sing this together. Since the Tallis' Canon tune can be sung as a round, try that with your first verse. Children enjoy rounds.

7. Write a first line for each prophecy. If you put blanks for each word or syllable, it is easier to fit in new words. Using the sample introductory verse, show how the words fit into the blanks:

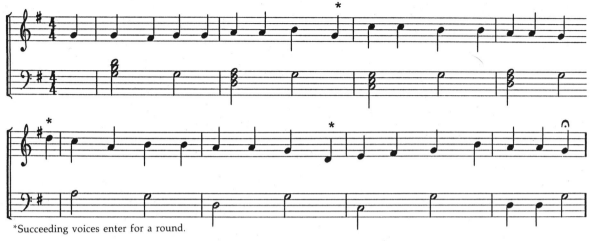

*Succeeding voices enter for a round.

The proph-ets spoke so long a-go

— — — — — — — —

— — — — — — — —

— — — — — — — —

Give each person the first line that corresponds with his or her assigned prophecy. Make sure that the prophecy is understood.

Some students will need help to complete their verses, but they learn a lot in the process. The assigned first lines should be as simple as possible.

First Line Suggestions

Verse 1: "The prophets spoke so long ago. . . ." (see above)

Verse 2: "When peace does come to Is-ra-el. . . ." (Isaiah 2:4)

Verse 3: "The wolf shall lie down with the kid. . . ." (Isaiah 11:6)

Verse 4: "From Beth-le-hem, the lit-tle town. . . ." (Micah 5:2–3)

Verse 5: "He'll be from Jesse's family. . . ." (Isaiah 11:1–3)

Verse 6: "A fair young maid shall bear a son. . . ." (Isaiah 7:14)

Verse 7: " 'A child is born' I-sai-ah said. . . ." (Isaiah 9:6–7)

Verse 8: "The Lord will bring his ho-ly light. . . ." (Isaiah 60:1–3)

Verse 9: "A righ-teous one shall reign as king. . . ." (Jeremiah 23:5)

Verse 10: "The Sav-ior Lord some-day will die. . . ." (Isaiah 53:3–7)

What results should you expect? Some will be very good. This is an excellent example of Isaiah 7:14:

A fair young maid shall bear a son.
And he will be the Holy One.
She'll call his name Im-man-u-el.
Messiah will save Is-ra-el.

Some will reflect the age of the "composer." For example, after reading Micah 5:2–3, one child wrote:

He is the cre-a-tor of all,
He won't be small. He will be tall.

For the best effect, it's wise not to tamper too much with the writers' wording unless they're too far "off-base."

Sing and Share

After we had put our ten verses together and sung them, we decided that we would like to share them with the congregation. We could invite them to sing our hymn, too!

Church Presentation

I explained to our congregation what the class had been studying. We handed out sheets that included the words of all ten verses, the Bible references, and the writers' names.

Junior choir members sang the introductory verse. Then each writer read his or her prophecy from the Bible. We had practiced this ahead of time, since if the children couldn't be heard, much would be lost.

After each two readings, the congregation sang the appropriate two verses and so on until the hymn was finished. The organist accompanied the singing.

I Don't Believe It

An Easy-to-Do Pageant

by Linda Poeima

Here is a Christmas pageant idea that is unbelievably easy and has proven successful. It requires no purchase of expensive scripts, no learning of lines, and no rehearsals. Any number of children or adults can participate.

All that is needed is a storyteller, an audience, simple pageant costumes (leftovers from former years work well), and the Christmas story as recorded in the Gospels of Matthew and Luke. Stage props would include a cardboard door for the inn, a couple of bales of hay, a manger with a baby, and a few chairs or boxes for angels and stars to stand on.

Possibly you are already saying, "I don't believe it." If so, you are ready to take part in this Christmas program.

As the audience arrives, the children are led to a coatrack where they can select the costumes of their choice. They are then seated in the front row of the congregation. When everyone is ready, the storyteller begins.

Long ago, in a small town called Nazareth, there lived a young girl named Mary. *(Choose an appropriately dressed child to come up front.)* She was only about fifteen years old. One evening while Mary was seated outside enjoying the cool night air, she was astounded when an angel appeared. The angel's name was Gabriel. *(Ask a child dressed in an angel costume to come forward.)* He told Mary that she had been chosen to have God's baby son. At first Mary was afraid. *(Ask Mary to look afraid.)* Then she fell on her knees. She might have shaken her head and said, "I don't believe it!" *(Ask Mary to repeat this line.)* But Gabriel put his hand on her shoulder and said, "Believe." *(Angel repeats this word.)* Then the angel disappeared while Mary thought about what had happened.

The story would continue much as it has been recorded in the Bible except that all the characters, at the appropriate times, repeat these two lines: "I don't believe it!" and "Believe!" Soon the actors will catch on, and little prompting will be needed. Here are some examples of scenes that could be included:

Mary shares her good news with Joseph, and he responds with, "I don't believe it." She replies, "Believe."

The angel assures Joseph that Mary is to have God's son, but again Joseph shouts, "I don't believe it," and the angel assures him with "Believe."

When Mary, heavy with child, mounts the little donkey, the donkey loudly brays, "I don't believe it," but Mary gently pats the donkey on the head and whispers, "Believe."

The innkeeper looks at Joseph and says, "I don't believe it," but Joseph points to Mary and states, "Believe."

At the stable, Mary looks in and sighs, "I don't believe it," but Joseph nods his head and mumbles, "Believe."

Of course, the shepherds on the hillside respond to the angels with, "We don't believe it," and the heavenly host sings, "Believe."

When the wise men note the new star in the heavens, they, too, declare, "We don't believe it," while the star twinkles back, "Believe."

Even the camels might grumble, "We don't believe it," when they are laden down with gold, myrrh, and frankincense, only to hear the wise men say, "Believe."

On the story goes, improvised by the storyteller with children spontaneously playing all the parts from Mary and Joseph to the donkey and the twinkling stars.

The story might end in this way:

When the visitors had ceased coming and the stable was again quiet, the cow and sheep looked into the manger, eager for a midnight snack. But on seeing the baby Jesus sleeping on the hay they, too, said, "We don't believe it." Then from all around them, from Mary and Joseph, the shepherds, the wise men, the angels, and the stars, they heard a loud and joyous "Believe!" *(All the cast repeats this line.)*

Today we, too, have the opportunity to proclaim the good news of Christ's birth. As the world around us declares, "I don't believe it," may we be quick to respond with a loud and confident "Believe" *(spoken by the entire congregation).*

I Had Forgotten Who I Am

by Garry L. Oliver

SANTA is dressed in a traditional Santa Claus costume. SAINT NICHOLAS, who is dressed in a red-and-white gown with a tall bishop's mitre on his head, must look ecclesiastical, yet relatively like Santa. A Christmas tree stands by the front of the sanctuary.

(SANTA enters through a side door. Looks around. Shrugs shoulders. Places a Santa doll under the Christmas tree along with a large candy cane. He hears something and dashes here and there frantically to escape notice by someone approaching. Finally, he hides behind the Christmas tree.)

SAINT NICHOLAS: *(Enters from the back of the sanctuary carrying a candlelighter ceremoniously to the front. After bowing, he lights the candles with a flair. He stands reverently for a moment in front of the altar or Communion table, straightening the altar cloth and candles. Sensing a presence, he suddenly looks up and around, alarmed.)* Who's there?

(SANTA *moves slightly and tries to become more inconspicuous behind the tree.*)

SAINT NICHOLAS: *(Notices the Santa doll beneath the tree. Picks it up and examines it wonderingly. Looks around again.)* Who is that? I know someone is here. Show yourself!

(SANTA *again tries to hide more deeply behind the tree.*)

SAINT NICHOLAS: *(Looks around, more determined now to find someone. Finally spies SANTA.)* There you are! What's going on here?

SANTA *(coming out sheepishly from behind the tree)*: I'm sorry. I thought you'd think I was a trespasser.

SAINT NICHOLAS: Well, aren't you? The door was locked, wasn't it?

SANTA: Well, I never use doors. I come down the chimney. Everybody knows that. I thought this was somebody's house, not a church . . . but I left a gift just the same! Please don't

be angry. Don't call the police. I'll leave as I came.

SAINT NICHOLAS: Of course, through the chimney, I presume! *(Looks intently at SANTA for a moment.)* Don't leave yet. Who are you?

SANTA *(rather astonished)*: Who? I'm Santa Claus! Everybody knows that.

SAINT NICHOLAS *(puzzled)*: Santa Claus?

SANTA: I'm Santa Claus . . . the Spirit of Christmas . . . bearer of Christmas gifts.

SAINT NICHOLAS: The what? The Spirit of Christmas . . . bearer of Christmas gifts? What is that? Do you . . . bring Christmas spirit to people?

SANTA *(looks a little embarrassed)*: Well, you might say that *(looks puzzled)*, though I don't think most people see me that way. I guess that might be true. Maybe . . . *(seems to remember something from the past)*.

29

SAINT NICHOLAS: What is that you are wearing? That red suit?

SANTA *(looks down at his suit)*: Oh, this . . . it's my regular Christmas Eve suit that I wear for bringing toys to children . . . and adults, if they want to see me. *(Looks at elbow.)* It's getting a little worn. Maybe I need to change into something else! *(Looks at SAINT NICHOLAS'S clothes.)* And what is that you're wearing? That is very classy. Where'd you get it?

SAINT NICHOLAS *(rather haughty and surprised)*: This? Why, it's my bishop's garb! I'm bishop of Myra . . . Nicholas!

SANTA: You look rather familiar . . . but the name Nicholas doesn't ring a bell. Haven't I seen you at Sears or Macy's this year?

SAINT NICHOLAS: I don't think so. But, as I was saying, I'm the bishop. These clothes represent my office.

SANTA: Your office . . . *(Looks as though he might remember something.)*

SAINT NICHOLAS: Why, yes! This mitre represents the priesthood. We have worn mitres since the Hebrews built the first temple at Jerusalem. My red gown symbolizes the blood of our Lord Jesus as it was spilled upon Golgotha. The white cuffs and collar are reminders of the purity that comes from accepting his cleansing sacrifice. We are whiter than snow now, Isaiah told us. These garments are worn as they were years ago, even though it is now the year of our Lord 325.

SANTA *(looks shocked)*: 325? It's 19_____ *(fill in the year this play is acted)*. *(Turns to audience.)* I must be dreaming!

SAINT NICHOLAS: What is that you say?

SANTA: Uhh . . . nothing . . . never mind!

SAINT NICHOLAS: Oh! Well, I usually carry a shepherd's crook. *(Makes the shape with his hand.)* I am one of Christ's undershepherds caring for the flock of God, the church.

SANTA *(excitedly)*: A shepherd's crook, huh? Looks kind of like this? *(Gets the candy cane from under the Christmas tree and holds it up for all to see.)* I've always wondered! It's red . . . and white, too! *(Continues to look at it in wonder.)*

SAINT NICHOLAS: That is strange! In many ways we look rather alike. *(Both face congregation standing side by side looking at each other in amazement.)*

SANTA: Hmmm . . . you look familiar to me. Where have I seen you before?

SAINT NICHOLAS: I have no idea, but one thing is certain—I must return here at eight sharp for services. This is Christmas Eve, you know!

SANTA: Why, certainly I know! That's why I'm here too . . . I suppose. You mind if I stay around a bit longer, and, you know, just think? I promise to leave pretty soon. And the deer are getting fidgety by this time, I'm sure.

SAINT NICHOLAS: The what? Deer? Why in the world do you have deer?

SANTA: They pull my sleigh . . . of course!

SAINT NICHOLAS: Sleigh? The chimney . . . up on the roof . . . *(sarcastically)* but, of course!

SANTA: It snows constantly at the North Pole. And, they're fine jumpers, you know. One bound and we can make it to New York City, Buenos Aires, or. . . . Oh, never mind! I see you don't understand what I'm talking about!

SAINT NICHOLAS *(shakes his head in disbelief)*: Oh, well . . . the world is made up of all kinds of people! When you leave, please pull the door shut behind you. It is cold out there, and wood is getting expensive nowadays. *(Starts to walk off but pauses and looks back.)* You will leave by the door, won't you?

SANTA: But my deer are on the roof! I guess I could go out through the door, climb up the downspout, and. . . .

SAINT NICHOLAS: Never mind! *(Chuckles out loud.)* Stay as long as you like . . . leave however you wish. *(Shakes his head.)*

SANTA: Thank you for your kindness. It was nice to meet you. I hope I see you again.

SAINT NICHOLAS: Yes, it was rather an unusual meeting . . . but nice! God's blessings upon you as you give tonight . . . the, uhhh . . . spirit of Christmas. I have always been fond of giving gifts to the poor and unfortunate, you know. Why, I remember the time during the flood when the children were trapped in the house without anything to eat for days. I went to them in a large tub . . . I couldn't find a boat. Anyway, when I got there, the water was still rising and about to go over the doorstep, so we just all got into the tub and floated back to safety. Then there was the time when I . . . *(Shakes his head and laughs.)* Ho, ho, ho! *(Lifts his hands in disbelief that he has gone on so.)* Ah, memories! An old man's folly! *(Returns to check the candles. Faces SANTA. Makes the sign of the cross.)*

(*Santa kneels.*)

Saint Nicholas: Go in peace. Serve the Lord. *(Departs up the aisle toward the door.)*

Santa: And you, Sir . . . God bless you! Go in peace. Serve the Lord. *(Startled.)*

Saint Nicholas *(turns back to look at* Santa, *also startled)*: You say that blessing with such authority. Have you been a priest?

Santa: It would make you wonder.

Saint Nicholas: Uhh . . . remember the door. Good night. *(Leaves by the same door he entered.)*

Santa: Why did I say that? It felt so natural. It seems that I have said it before. *(Looks around. Sits in the pastor's chair to think. Strokes his beard. Feels the arms of the chair, remembering. Walks to the altar or Communion table and looks at it as if remembering something. Picks up the articles lying on the altar one by one. Feels them, remembering something.)* I believe I remember . . . Myra . . . red robe . . . *(touches his red suit)* . . . white cuffs . . . collar . . . shepherd's crook . . . mitre *(touches his red hat)* . . . I do declare! I think . . . I think I am Saint Nicholas. I am Saint Nicholas! I am Saint Nicholas, too! *(Pauses.)* I had forgotten who I am. I had forgotten who I am! I am Saint Nicholas of Myra. I had forgotten. *(Stands firmly now in front of the altar handling the objects there in a familiar fashion, with a dignified air of confidence. Slowly kneels before the altar, remaining there for several moments. Removes his hat in reverence. Rises slowly. Places his hat back on his head and turns around to leave. Stops. Looks back at the altar. Looks at the Santa doll beneath the Christmas tree. Slowly goes to the tree, picks up the doll, and with reverence and care places it upon the altar. Stops while straightening the altar to ponder what he has done. Goes to the tree again, picks up the candy, and takes it to the altar, placing it next to the Santa doll. Leaves quickly through the side door through which he first entered. In the distance he hears laughing.)* Ho, ho, ho!

This brief drama might be used on the second Sunday in Advent. For more information about Nicholas, the Bishop of Myra, see the article "Does Santa Belong in Church?"

The Best Christmas Ever

A Christmas Play

by Kathryn Choy-Wong

Notes to the Teacher

The following play takes place in an urban setting with a multicultural flavor. The purpose of the play is to introduce the ethnic diversity in the United States and to affirm the different cultural celebrations of the birth of Jesus Christ. Also underlying the play are universal lessons of giving, self-sacrifice, and the true meaning of Christmas.

The play can be easily adapted to fit your own cultural heritage and background. This is simply done by changing the names and situations of the main character, Simon, his family, as well as some specific details. We suggest, however, that the other characters be left as they are. They will add to the variety in the play.

If you want to adapt the play, you might change the following names and places: Simon and his family; the name of the Commodore Stockton Elementary School; the Chinese restaurant, Chinese language school, and some of the Chinese language in the dialogue; Mr. Lew's sewing factory; the kinds of food; and reference to the Chinese Bible.

CHARACTERS

NARRATOR
MRS. CHEW (a young woman)
FRANK ONO (a ten-year-old boy)
SARAH MCALLISTER (a ten-year-old girl)
AMOS WEBSTER (a ten-year-old boy)
PEDRO RAMÍREZ (a ten-year-old boy)
SIMON WONG (a ten-year-old boy)
MRS. WONG (a middle-aged woman)
MR. WONG (a middle-aged man)
MAY WONG (an eight-year-old girl)
TREE SALESMAN (a middle-aged man)
MRS. HO (an elderly woman)

SCENE 1

Scene 1 opens with the children, except MAY WONG, sitting facing MRS. CHEW. The NARRATOR is on one side of the stage or play area. This is where the NARRATOR will remain during the entire play. Props may be used if desired and may be as simple or as elaborate as desired.

NARRATOR: Scene 1 takes place at Commodore Stockton Elementary school in San Francisco's Chinatown. We find Simon Wong, Pedro Ramírez, Sarah McAllister, Frank Ono, and Amos Webster in Mrs. Chew's fifth grade class. The children are sitting at their desks facing Mrs. Chew and the chalkboard.

MRS. CHEW: Jo sun! Good morning, children.

CHILDREN: Good morning, Mrs. Chew.

MRS. CHEW: This week I have a surprise for you. We are going to make something very special for a very special holiday. Does anyone know what that holiday is?

(All the children raise their hands.)

MRS. CHEW: Frank?

FRANK: Christmas, of course! Everybody knows that.

MRS. CHEW: Yes, Frank. So in preparation for Christmas, we will make something special. I want the class to decide what it would like to make. Do you have any suggestions?

SARAH: Let's make Christmas trees out of pages from *Reader's Digest.* We can paint them green and make little ornaments.

AMOS: We could make Christmas cards for Mom, Dad, Grandpa, and Grandma.

PEDRO: Let's make a piñata, fill it with candy, and then break it in class!

FRANK: Yeah! That sounds neat. And if we make Christmas trees too, we can hang candy canes

32

as ornaments. And if we make Christmas cards, we can put little Christmas candies inside the envelopes!

SARAH: All you ever want to do, Frank, is eat candy!

MRS. CHEW: Simon, you haven't suggested anything. What would you like the class to make?

SIMON: I dunno. It doesn't matter.

MRS. CHEW: Well, children, these have all been good suggestions. Let's do some more thinking about it tomorrow. Right now, we need to do our lessons.

CHILDREN (faces grimacing): Aw-w-w-w.

MRS. CHEW: Take out your history books, children.

SCENE 2

NARRATOR: Scene 2 takes place in the school playground during lunch time. Everyone is eating. The children are excited because Christmas is coming. They talk animatedly about the holiday season.

FRANK: I can't wait until Christmas. I get to eat all those candy canes on our Christmas tree. And then, I get all those great Christmas presents. I already hinted to Mom and Dad that I wanted a spaceship for Christmas. They'll probably get it. Of course, they'll say it's from Santa.

PEDRO: I can't wait either. In our house, we have a piñata on Christmas Eve. All my cousins come over and join us. My parents fill the piñata with candy and toys. We have a lot of fun. We even get to help make the piñata. Then we go to early mass on Christmas morning.

AMOS: We don't have that, but we have just as much fun. Grandpa and Grandma have the whole family over for Christmas Eve. We play games all night, sing, and tell stories. Then at midnight Grandpa tells us the Christmas story. After that, Grandpa and Grandma give us a special Christmas present, which is always something they make themselves.

PEDRO: What do you do, Simon?

SIMON (looking downcast): Not much. We don't really do anything special.

FRANK: Nothing? You don't have a Christmas tree?

SIMON (eyes looking down and distant): No.

PEDRO: Not even presents?

SIMON (voice gets more distant): No.

AMOS: You don't sing? Or play games? Or tell stories?

SIMON (almost whispering): No.

(The boys shake their heads sadly at SIMON. The bell rings and lunch time is over.)

AMOS (in disgust): Well, we'd better go to class. I can't wait until Christmas vacation.

SCENE 3

NARRATOR: Scene 3 takes place in a Chinese restaurant. Simon runs in. Mr. Wong is cooking. Mrs. Wong is cleaning a table. May Wong is doing her homework on the counter.

SIMON: Hi, Baba! Hi, Mama! Hi, Sis!

MRS. WONG: How are you today, Son? Did you have a good day at school?

SIMON: School was okay.

MRS. WONG: Well, have a snack and do your homework right away. Remember, you and May have to go to Chinese language school in a little while. Also, after Chinese school, remember to pick up some groceries for Mrs. Ho. She's not feeling so well today.

SIMON: Yes, Mama. (Sits on the counter staring into space. Doesn't touch his snack or his homework.)

MRS. WONG: What's wrong, Simon? You sick?

SIMON: No. (Then, hesitantly.) Mama? Do you think we can have a Christmas tree this Christmas? We've never had one.

MRS. WONG: A tree? Why? You know we can't afford to buy one. And of what use is the tree, and a dead tree at that!

SIMON: I know. But I thought we could have one just this once. Everyone at school has one.

MRS. WONG: Well, you're not everyone. If everyone has a million dollars, do you expect to have a million dollars? Now, no more nonsense.

SIMON: Yes, Mama.

SCENE 4

NARRATOR: Scene 4 takes place on the way to Chinese school. May and Simon are walking together.

SIMON: I wish Mama and Baba would change their minds about getting a tree.

MAY: I know. Everyone has a tree. We go to school and there's a tree in the auditorium. We go to church and there's a tree in the social hall. We go to Chinese school and there's a tree. I don't see why we can't have one. They don't cost that much, do they?

SIMON: I dunno. *(He pauses. Suddenly a smile comes across his once-sad face.)* I have an idea! Maybe you and I can get a tree. Why don't we get it for Mama and Baba as a present? Why do we have to expect them to get everything for us all the time? And I heard they're cheaper on Christmas Eve. Maybe we can get a special price.

MAY: How are we going to do that? We don't have any allowance like our classmates do.

SIMON: Maybe I can do some errands for Mrs. Lee at the grocery store. She needs someone to help her deliver groceries to some of her customers.

MAY: And maybe I can do some chores for Mr. Lew at the sewing factory, since Mama used to work there.

SIMON: And tonight, on the way home we can check on the price of a Christmas tree.

(The two run off happily to Chinese school.)

SCENE 5

NARRATOR: Scene 5 takes place on Christmas Eve. Simon and May meet outside the Christmas tree lot. They are counting their money.

MAY: How much have you got, Simon? I've got three dollars.

SIMON: I've got four dollars. I think we may have enough. The man said the trees are cheaper on Christmas Eve.

MAY: Good, let's go in.

(They walk into the Christmas tree lot.)

SIMON: Sir, we would like to buy a tree. How much is your cheapest tree?

TREE SALESMAN: Well, the cheapest we have left is this tree. It'll cost you ten dollars.

(MAY and SIMON look disappointed.)

MAY: Ten dollars!

TREE SALESMAN *(feeling sorry for them)*: Well, how much do you have?

SIMON: Seven dollars.

TREE SALESMAN: Well, tell you what. I'll let you take this tree for eight dollars. You can owe me the dollar and pay me back later. You look like kids I can trust. In fact, if you help me clean up this place a little, you don't owe me anything.

SIMON and MAY: That's a deal!

SCENE 6

NARRATOR: Scene 6 takes place at Mr. and Mrs. Wong's apartment building. It is now 6 P.M. on Christmas Eve. Simon and May walk into their building with great big smiles on their faces. They are carrying the tree. They pass by their neighbor's apartment and see Mrs. Ho sitting alone, talking to herself and listening to Chinese music. Simon and May remember that Mrs. Ho's husband died a year ago and that she doesn't have any children. Simon and May whisper to each other.

SIMON *(whispering)*: Let's give Mrs. Ho the Christmas tree.

MAY *(whispering)*: Yeah, and then offer to help her decorate it later tonight.

SIMON: Mrs. Ho, we'd like to give you this Christmas tree. Merry Christmas!

MRS. HO *(tears in her eyes)*: You two are so nice and thoughtful to remember an old woman like me. Thank you for this beautiful tree.

MAY: We'll come and help you decorate the tree tonight, Mrs. Ho, if you'd like us to.

SIMON: Yes, May and I made some nice ornaments at school. They'll look good on the tree.

MRS. HO *(happily)*: And I have some old cloth and ribbons we can use.

MAY *(excited)*: I can't wait.

SIMON: We'll see you later, Mrs. Ho. Joy geen, until later.

MAY: Joy geen, see you later.

(SIMON and MAY leave MRS. HO. They walk to their own apartment and stand outside their door.)

SIMON: I wanted that tree for Mama and Baba, but I'm glad to give it to Mrs. Ho. Let's not tell Mama and Baba about it. They might feel bad that we didn't get a tree after all.

MAY: Agreed.

(SIMON and MAY enter their own apartment, beaming with happiness.)

MR. WONG: Glad to see you two happy. Mama and I have a surprise for you.

MRS. WONG *(smiling)*: Yes, we wanted to keep it a secret. You two have been such good children, and since it is a religious holiday, we decided to prepare a special dinner. We cooked all your favorite foods . . . shark fin soup, pressed duck, thousand layer buns, Chinese mushrooms, and steak cubes!

(The children are wide-eyed and speechless.)

MR. WONG (smiling): Well, what do you say?

SIMON (regaining his speech): It's the most delicious dinner I have ever seen. Thank you!

MAY: This dinner must have cost a fortune! How can we afford it? All my favorite foods—thank you both!

MRS. WONG: Well, we just saved our money. We wanted to do something very special for you two.

MR. WONG: After dinner, we can spend the evening together. Mama can read the Christmas story to you from her Chinese Bible. Then we can go to church for the Christmas Eve service.

SIMON: Sounds great. But do you think we can invite Mrs. Ho? She's so lonely. We can help her celebrate this holiday. She also has a tree and can't decorate it all by herself. Can we all help her decorate it?

MRS. WONG: I think that is an excellent idea!

SIMON (beaming): We never had a Christmas Eve dinner before. We're not usually all here on Christmas Eve. Now we have our whole family together—and even Mrs. Ho! This is the best Christmas I ever had! Happy Christmas Eve, everyone!

No Room on Riverview Boulevard

by Karen Hetrick

CAST (in order of appearance):

GEORGE (Martin's guest)
MARTIN (youth group president)
BARB (cynical youth group member)
WILSON (cold youth group member)
MELISSA (persistent youth group member)
MAID (at house #1)
OLD MAN (at house #2)
PARTY GUESTS, OPTIONAL (at house #3)
WOMAN (at house #4)
HER HUSBAND (at house #4)
SOCIALITE (at house #5)
MRS. CRISMAN (at house #6)
MR. CRISMAN (at house #6)

The principal characters of GEORGE, MARTIN, BARB, WILSON, and MELISSA can be played by any combination of male or female actors by simply changing the names accordingly.

SETTING: A street in a neighborhood of homes on a snowy evening near Christmas. The street is lined with five houses, with a sixth smaller house apart from the others but in a central location. All action takes place outside the doors of the houses with an additional interior scene at the sixth house.

STAGING: The houses can be portrayed in a variety of ways. For example:

1. A wooden, cardboard, or cloth backdrop with houses painted on it. Doors need to open on houses 1, 4, 5, and 6. A window opens or a curtain is drawn aside on house #2. House #3 needs a window that can be seen through if the optional party guests are used.

2. A separate backdrop for each house with the same openings mentioned above.

3. One backdrop of one house with a movable door and window that can be changed slightly to portray the different homes. For instance, someone could reach around and change the house number each time, or add or subtract Christmas lights.

4. Another approach would be to use more of the auditorium or sanctuary than just the stage or platform. For example, the first house would be the door to a side room at the left of the platform. The second house could be staged at the balcony with the carolers standing below the "second-story window." The third house could be positioned at the back of the sanctuary, and so on. Each sanctuary or fellowship hall will present unique approaches that could heighten audience interest. The entrance of the sixth house will need to be on or near the platform since that house is central to the drama.

PROPS: GEORGE, MARTIN, BARB, WILSON and MELISSA need coats, scarves, mittens, and carol books; this group will need two flashlights.

> MAID: Apron and or cap
> OLD MAN: bathrobe and long, pointed nightcap
> WOMAN: lounging robe and bowl
> HUSBAND: newspaper and bowl
> SOCIALITE: good coat and hat, fur if possible
> MRS. CRISMAN: shawl
> MR. CRISMAN: old sweater

For the interior of the Crisman's house: two easy chairs, one or two straight chairs, tray with seven cups, small Christmas tree with Chrismons tinted to look like wood, wood stove or fireplace (made of cardboard and spray painted).

SPECIAL EFFECTS

1. You may want to provide optional lighting in the stove or fireplace that could be dimmed or unplugged on cue.

2. If you do not have people acting as party guests at house #3, you can make a tape of muf-

ed secular Christmas music and background voices. The tape could be turned up and faded back down on cue. If cast members are used, they will need to practice merrymaking in varying degrees of volume as the focus shifts to and from house #3.

PLAYING TIME: Approximately fifteen minutes.

(Curtain opens. GEORGE, MARTIN, BARB, WILSON, and MELISSA enter stage left or from back side aisle of sanctuary; they pause.)

GEORGE: One more block and we're there. What a great idea. Do you do this every year?

MARTIN: Thanks. No, this is a first. We always drive through to see the lights and decorations. *(They walk on as he continues.)* But I figured what better way to see them than to come caroling with the youth group?

(They pause again, heads swiveling slowly a time or two, as if waiting for traffic to pass.)

BARB: That's Martin. Always thinking of ways to spread Christmas cheer.

MARTIN: Well—you might say it's two-way cheer. We sing beautiful Christmas songs for poor, lonely, rich people, and they cheer us by inviting us into their homes.

BARB: And maybe throwing us some crumbs from their holiday baking.

MARTIN *(innocently)*: Now that you mention it. . . .

(They approach the first house and stop beside it.)

WILSON *(rubs his arms)*: Let's get started. It's cold out here.

(They open carol books.)

MELISSA: How about "Silent Night"?

MARTIN: Nah. Something peppy. How about "Joy to the World"?

(They sing one verse loudly with enthusiasm.)

MAID *(opens the door far enough to stick her head out)*: Madame asks that you kindly move on. You're making it impossible for her to hear the "Perry Como Forty-third Annual Christmas Special" on television. *(Closes door.)*

BARB *(in same huffy tone as the maid)*: Well, lah-dee-dah!

MARTIN: Down, Barb. We'll just go where we're wanted. On to the next house.

(They move toward house #2.)

WILSON *(shivering)*: Br-r-r, it's cold.

MELISSA *(tries her suggestion again)*: How about "Silent Night"?

MARTIN *(puts her off again)*: Later. Let's try "O Come, All Ye Faithful."

(As they sing the line "Come and behold Him," they are interrupted by the OLD MAN.)

OLD MAN *(leaning out open window)*: Scram, you brats! You woke me up!

MARTIN *(aside to group)*: At 7:30? *(To OLD MAN.)* Sorry, sir. Merry Christmas.

OLD MAN: Bah! Humbug! *(Slams down window.)*

GEORGE: Every street has its Scrooge. *(They approach house #3 with muffled music and party sounds filtering out.)* This house looks more promising. *(He peers through the window. If real party guests are used, they should be visible to the audience through the window.)* There must be fifty people in there!

MELISSA *(tries a more direct hint)*: "Silent Night" is on page 16.

MARTIN *(snaps at her)*: We'll get to it. *(Leafs through book.)* OK. Page 24—"The First Noel."

(As they sing one verse, the party noise increases, drowning them out.)

BARB: It's a zoo in there. They can't even hear us.

(They turn away from the house, and the party sounds diminish.)

GEORGE: We're all practiced up, anyway.

(Group stands in front of house #4.)

MELISSA *(hopefully)*: Is it—?

MARTIN *(interrupts)*: Not yet. Let's try "Away in a Manger."

(They sing one verse. A couple comes to the door to listen. They are both holding bowls. He has a newspaper in one hand.)

WOMAN: Thank you so much. We're sorry we can't invite you in. We just had our carpet steam-cleaned this afternoon. There would be so much mess tracked in. . . . You understand.

HUSBAND: Yeah, what a shame. We were just having some ice cream.

WILSON *(to Melissa)*: He's gotta be kidding.

MARTIN: No problem. Have a merry Christmas.

WOMAN and HUSBAND *(together)*: Merry Christmas! *(They close the door.)*

(Group turns away from house #4 to house #5.)

GEORGE: I have a feeling our luck is going to change at this place.

MARTIN: Let's sing "We Three Kings." Wilson, you start us off.

WILSON *(through clenched teeth and standing ramrod straight)*: I can't. My lips are frozen.

(Before they can begin to sing, a fur-coated woman comes out the door and closes it behind her.)

SOCIALITE: May I help you?

MARTIN: We were about to sing some Christmas carols for you.

SOCIALITE: How sweet. What a pity I don't have time to listen. I'm on my way out. Only seven shopping days till Christmas, you know. Between the parties and the concerts. . . . If only you could come back around January fifth or so, I'm sure I won't be so busy then. *(Looks away toward drive.)* My husband has the car warmed up. Happy holidays. *(She exits.)*

ALL: Happy holidays. *(They huddle in a tight group, looking dejected.)*

GEORGE: I'm sure the next house—

BARB *(cuts him off)*: Open your eyes, Mr. Optimist. There is no next house. We're fresh out of houses!

WILSON *(tries to look disappointed)*: Doggone. (Brightens.) We could go back to my house and soak our feet in hot chocolate.

MELISSA *(asserts herself)*: Nothing doing. *(To MARTIN.)* You said we could sing "Silent Night." I brought the songbooks and the flashlights, and I'm not leaving until we sing "Silent Night" to someone!

MARTIN: OK, OK! We'll find a house.

BARB: Oh sure. From here to the river there's nothing but woods. And beyond that is the golf course.

MARTIN *(to MELISSA)*: We could sing to the golfers who might be out with those glow-in-the-dark orange balls.

WILSON: That's not funny.

GEORGE: Wait. On around this curve there's a small place that used to be a gatehouse for one of the large homes.

(They approach house #6.)

MARTIN: It's worth a try.

(In front of this much humbler dwelling they sing "Silent Night." As they sing, an older couple comes to the door to listen.)

MRS. CRISMAN: Lovely. Let's hear some more.

MR. CRISMAN: But don't stand out in the cold. Come in; come in.

GEORGE *(to BARB as they tramp inside)*: Told you.

(They shed their coats.)

WILSON: These are my kind of people.

MR. CRISMAN: Sit down, sit down. I'm afraid we're short on chairs.

MARTIN: No problem, sir. Some of us can sit on the floor by the wood stove.

WILSON: I'll sacrifice my chair and sit on the hard floor. *(Rushes to the stove.)*

(MELISSA takes the straight chair. Other carolers sit in easy chairs or on the floor in front of the stove.)

MR. CRISMAN *(sits in easy chair)*: Mother and I were just commenting on how lonely it is at Christmas with the grandchildren so far away.

MRS. CRISMAN: Sing another verse. I have water heating for tea. We'll share a favorite treat of ours—hot spiced sassafras tea. *(She exits to the kitchen.)*

BARB *(aside to MARTIN)*: Oh no!

MARTIN *(calls after MRS. CRISMAN)*: We'd enjoy that. *(Aside to BARB.)* Enjoy it. That's an order.

(Carolers sing last verse of "Silent Night.")

MRS. CRISMAN *(enters with a tray of cups)*: Help me pass the tea, Father.

(MR. CRISMAN takes them from the tray, handing them to the carolers. MRS. CRISMAN sits in her own chair.)

GEORGE: Your tree is pretty.

MR. CRISMAN: We can't have a large one. But I carved all the ornaments myself.

WILSON *(looks more closely)*: They're Chrismons, aren't they?

MRS. CRISMAN: Yes, indeed. We want our tree to remind us of Christ and his life when we look at it.

MR. CRISMAN: The dreary December days remind us of the time before Jesus was born—how dark life must have looked to humankind.

BARB: But he was born.

MRS. CRISMAN: So he was. And we want our Christmas each year to be a bright spot just as the new baby must have been so long ago.

GEORGE: Especially to the few who saw past the baby to the king.

(Pause as stove "coals" dim or a clock chimes.)

MARTIN *(checks watch)*: Look at the time. We gotta go.

(They get up and put on their coats.)

MRS. CRISMAN *(helps tie a scarf or two)*: We're delighted you came by to share some cheer with us.

BARB: And thank you for sharing yours. *(Looks meaningfully at MARTIN.)*

(Outside they turn and sing "We Wish You a Merry Christmas.")

MR. CRISMAN: Thank you.

MRS. CRISMAN: A blessed Christmas to you. *(She closes the door. The group walks away slowly.)*

GEORGE: That was fun.

MELISSA: I'm glad I "suggested" it.

WILSON: What warm-hearted people. Sassafras tea never tasted so good.

BARB: It probably never will again either.

MARTIN *(looks back, and the group stops)*: Look—there they are waving at the window. *(They wave back.)* Is it my imagination, or is the porch light shining brighter than when we came?

BARB *(exasperated)*: Oh, really, Martin!

WILSON *(loosens scarf)*: I'm warm now, but it's too late for more caroling.

(Carolers approach their exit, pausing nearby for GEORGE and MARTIN to speak.)

GEORGE *(to MARTIN)*: Sorry your plan for caroling didn't work out.

MARTIN: Not at all. *(Gestures back toward house #6.)* Our visit to the Crismans more than made up for all the others who turned us away!

Journey to Bethlehem

by Renee Kaufman

Journey to Bethlehem is a service in seven scenes. The congregation meets together in the sanctuary for the first and last scenes while the other five take place in different, dimly lit areas of the church building. In separate rooms a portion of the Christmas story is pantomimed while the appropriate Scripture is read. (Choose whatever translation you prefer.) The scenes are designed to take similar lengths of time. Music for each scene may be presented by individuals or small groups or sung by the worshipers. As each scene is completed, the guide leads his or her group to the next destination.

The program begins with a hymn, an invocation, and a brief explanation of the process of the progressive service. The congregation is divided into five groups, each with a designated guide whom they are to follow throughout the service. It is suggested that silence be maintained while on the journey through dimly lit halls.

After the first scene, group 1 follows its guide to begin the journey. Carol singing and/or other appropriate activities take place as groups 2, 3, 4, and 5 await their turns.

The last scene does not begin until all five groups have gathered together in the sanctuary. Organ music, live or taped, may be played, or other special music provided until all the travelers have returned. *Journey to Bethlehem* is a different way to tell the Christmas story. Details of the service may be changed, but the idea of the journey (that is, physically moving to different locations) is one you may wish to use.

Opening Worship

Hymn
Invocation
Brief Explanation

Scene 1—Luke's Introduction

(This scene calls for a person dressed as Luke.)

NARRATION: Luke 1:1–4

DRAMA: Luke enters and sits at a table. He begins writing on a scroll with a quill pen.

Scene 2—The Annunciation

(For this scene two persons portray Mary and the angel Gabriel. The room is decorated with some furnishings to resemble a home.)

NARRATION: Luke 1:26–38

DRAMA: As the group enters the room, Mary is seated and working with a piece of cloth. Gabriel enters through a door. As Gabriel speaks, Mary acts startled, rises from her seat, and begins moving away from Gabriel. She stops when he reassures her. Mary acts puzzled when the question "How shall this be . . . ?" is read. Mary kneels at Gabriel's feet when her confession is read ("I am the handmaid of the Lord . . ."). The actors remain in this position during the music and as the guide leads the group of worshipers out of the room.

MUSIC: "O Come, O Come, Emmanuel!"

Scene 3—Mary Visits Elizabeth

(This scene, also set in a room with home furnishings, has two persons acting out the parts of Mary and Elizabeth.)

NARRATION: Luke 1:39–56

DRAMA: As the worshipers enter the room, Elizabeth appears to be preparing food at a table. Mary enters and Elizabeth rises to meet her. They embrace. They move to the table, are seated, and continue conversing. Mary is the only one speaking during the reading of the "Magnificat" (vv. 46–55).

MUSIC: "Come, Thou Long-Expected Jesus"

Scene 4—Arrival at Bethlehem

(Mary, Joseph, and the innkeeper are in this scene. The set is decorated to resemble a small inn.)

NARRATION: Luke 2:1, 3–7

DRAMA: Mary and Joseph enter and knock on the inn door. The innkeeper opens the door and Joseph indicates that they would like a room. The innkeeper shakes his head no. As Mary and Joseph prepare to leave, the innkeeper motions for them to wait. He points out the stable, and Mary and Joseph head in that direction.

MUSIC: "No Room" (from the cantata *Night of Miracles* by John W. Peterson, published by Singspiration, Inc.)

Scene 5—Announcement to the Shepherds

(The setting is a hillside in Judea, so a variety of props are used to portray this scene. Or it could be set outside, weather permitting.)

NARRATION: Luke 2:8–15

DRAMA: The shepherds are lying on the ground as the worshipers enter. The shepherds jump to their feet and begin backing away from the angels that enter. As the angels leave, the shepherds gesture excitedly as if talking with one another and then hurriedly leave.

MUSIC: "Hark! the Herald Angels Sing" or "Angels We Have Heard on High"

Scene 6—The Wise Men

(Herod and wise men are in this scene. Extra people portray chief priests, scribes, and palace guards. The setting is Herod's palace; a pulpit chair is used for the throne.)

NARRATION: Matthew 2:1–8

DRAMA: As the worshipers enter the room, Herod is sitting on his throne. The wise men enter and approach the throne. After hearing the wise men's question, Herod rises and motions for the wise men to come closer. He pantomimes telling them to travel to Bethlehem, find the Christ child, and return to him. The wise men then leave.

MUSIC: "We Three Kings of Orient Are" or "Star of the East"

Scene 7—The Nativity

(The sanctuary is dimly lit. Mary and Joseph are sitting by the manger watching the baby as the worshipers enter. Individuals are given candles before they are seated.)

DRAMA: (The actors playing Mary and Joseph are different from scene 4.) The angels from the previous scenes enter and stand behind Mary and Joseph. The shepherds enter from the rear of the sanctuary and approach the manger. They show their reverence for the Christ child and then move to one side of the manger. The wise men enter with gifts which they place around the manger. These characters remain in their places and keep their attention focused on the Christ child until the singing of "Silent Night, Holy Night" when they join in.

MUSIC: Solo—"Sweet Little Jesus Boy"

Following the solo, "Silent Night, Holy Night" is played. Youth move up the aisles lighting candles of the congregation. When all candles are lit, everyone stands and joins in the singing of "Silent Night, Holy Night." The congregation begins to exit while still singing.

What Christmas Is

by William D. Wolfe

CHARACTERS

    HENRY BROWNSTEAD—a middle-aged man
    HELEN BROWNSTEAD—a middle-aged woman
    STEPHANIE—a high school sophomore
    DAVID—a college freshman
    JOSEPH—a young adult
    MARY—a pregnant woman

PROPS

    Christmas tree and ornaments
    Couch and two chairs
    Clipboard with papers
    Two suitcases
    Quilt
    Wrapped Christmas packages
    Cookie container

Act I

SETTING: The action takes place in the living room of the Brownstead's home on December 21. There is a couch on the left side of the stage and two chairs on the right side. Boxes of Christmas decorations are in one of the chairs. In the center back is a Christmas tree, partially decorated. As the lights come on, HENRY is standing a few feet away from the tree with another ornament in his hand, admiring the tree.

HENRY: Helen! *(Pause.)* Helen!

HELEN *(rushing in from the right)*: What is it, Henry? I'm right in the middle of making Rudolphs.

HENRY: Rudolphs?

HELEN: Cookies. Rudolph-shaped cookies, Henry.

HENRY: Oh, well, just look at the tree for a minute. Isn't it a beauty?

HELEN *(walks from one side to the other and back again, looking at the tree)*: It looks OK to me. *(As she exits.)* I've got to get back to my cookies.

STEPHANIE *(enters from right, holding a clipboard)*: Hi, Dad! I've finished my Christmas list, and I'd like to go over these gift suggestions with you.

HENRY: What do you have there, a book?

STEPHANIE: No, Dad, it's just a few things I'd like for Christmas, ranked in order of priority and need.

HENRY: Let me see it. *(He takes the clipboard from her and looks at it a few seconds).* Your number one need is tickets to the Bruce Springsteen concert?

STEPHANIE: Yes, but they don't necessarily have to be the best seats!

HENRY: What's this? The Unfriendly Morticians?

STEPHANIE: Oh, that's a really with-it rock group. They have a new album out that is unreal.

HENRY: And you rate needing this album above needing some new socks, gym shoes, and school clothes?

STEPHANIE: Well, Dad! Everybody already has the album! I'm really behind!

HENRY: If everybody already has the album, borrow it. *(He hands the clipboard back to her.)*

STEPHANIE: OK. If you don't want me to get that album, that's all right. I'll sacrifice that idea.

HENRY: Stephanie, the spirit of Christmas is to be giving, not receiving.

STEPHANIE: I know, Dad. I just thought I would save you a lot of time shopping by telling you what I want. You know, allowing you to give those things that I really need, not things that I don't want.

HENRY: Stephanie, you're not hearing me.

STEPHANIE: Yes, I am.

HENRY: No, you're not. The spirit of Christmas is to focus on the needs of other people, not on yourself. Everything you have here is for you. Don't you think it's kind of selfish to hand someone a checklist of things you want and say, "Go to it, Dad?"

STEPHANIE: Maybe so.

HENRY: I don't mean to get down on you, honey, but there are a lot of people in the world who don't even have a bed to sleep in, let alone tickets to a Springs concert.

STEPHANIE: Springsteen, Dad! You know, "The Boss"!

HENRY: Springsteen, sorry! Anyway, Steph, what I'm trying to get across to you is that Christmas is meant to be more of a giving time than getting. Try to look at it that way.

STEPHANIE: I'm trying to look at it that way, Dad, but it's so totally un-American.

HENRY: Un-American?

STEPHANIE: Yeah, you know! Looking out for Number One! Getting the pay increase you want, or going on strike. Baseball players tired of only making a couple hundred thousand, asking for a tripling of their salaries, resulting in ticket prices going up for everyone else. U.S. corporations exploiting Third World labor by paying sub-poverty wages. Things like that!

HENRY: Stephanie, how do you know all these things?

STEPHANIE: I read the papers, Dad. After all, I am a sophomore this year.

HENRY: I'm afraid to see what you'll be saying when you're a senior.

STEPHANIE: Well, all those things are true, aren't they?

HENRY: Maybe . . . er . . . yes, but not everybody's that way. Believe it or not, there are a few decent, morally sound people in this world.

STEPHANIE: Like the Reverend George Jefferies?

HENRY: Now, Stephanie, you can't use him as an example.

STEPHANIE: Why not? You're the one who said he was as close to God as the apostle Paul. Then he suddenly disappears with the $200,000 the church had in savings.

HENRY: OK. I was wrong about him. I admit he had me fooled.

STEPHANIE: Well, it's just hard to be giving when most of the people you see around you are receiving. *(HELEN reenters.)*

HELEN: The cookies are finally in the oven. This is the last year I'm making those foolish Rudolphs!

STEPHANIE: You said that last year, Mom.

HELEN: Well, this time I mean it. How's the tree coming, Henry?

HENRY: I'm not nearly done yet.

HELEN: Please hurry it up! David will be getting home any time now, and I want the tree to be done when he gets here.

HENRY: OK, OK! Steph, give me a hand with these ornaments.

STEPHANIE *(begins to put ornaments on tree)*: I never thought I would be able to say this, but it will be good to have my big brother home again!

HENRY: Well, three months away from him will do that to you.

STEPHANIE: I still remember all the fights we used to get into, but I really do miss him. *(HENRY and STEPH continue adding ornaments until DAVID enters from the left side.)*

DAVID: Hi, everybody!

HENRY: David, you're home! *(Goes over to DAVID, shakes his hand, and gives him a big hug.)*

DAVID: Hi, Steph!

STEPHANIE: Hi, big brother! *(She gives him a hug.)*

DAVID *(steps back after hugging her and looks at her closely)*: Steph, you're looking like a real fox!

STEPHANIE: Oh, David! *(HELEN enters from the right.)*

DAVID: Hi, Mom!

HELEN: Oh, David, it's so good to have you home! *(Goes to him and hugs him.)* And you even wore nice clothes!

DAVID: Just for you, Mom.

HELEN: You're such a good boy, David. I can tell that college has taught you a lot.

DAVID: Yeah . . . sure . . . but it's sure good to be home.

HENRY: Well, son, we're glad you're here. I'm sure that this will be an extra special Christmas because you're back with us. How was the trip home?

DAVID: Pretty good. In fact, I brought a couple of people with me—a couple of friends of mine. What are the chances of their spending the night here with us?

HENRY: Well, David, I wish you had told us earlier.

HELEN: Now Henry! Any college friends of David's are welcome here. Don't be so reserved. Bring the boys in, David. I'll get the extra bedroom ready.

DAVID: Mom, they aren't all guys, and they aren't from college.

STEPHANIE: That's all right, David. Dad was just telling me that the purpose of Christmas is to give to others.

DAVID: Good, I'll go get them. *(He rushes out.)*

HENRY: Stephanie, I wasn't talking about things like this when I mentioned the purpose of Christmas.

STEPHANIE: Gee, Dad, it seems like a pretty Christmasy thing to me.

HELEN: Henry, I'm sure it will work out . . . I think.

STEPHANIE: Yeah, this might be kind of fun. *(DAVID reenters from left with MARY, who is visibly pregnant, and JOSEPH. All eyes are on MARY. HENRY and HELEN look stunned.)*

DAVID: Mom, Dad, Steph, these are my two good friends I met at the bus station in Roanoke. This is Joseph, and this is—

HENRY: Let me guess! This is Mary!

MARY: Pleased to meet you, Mr. Brownstead. *(All shake hands.)*

STEPHANIE: Wow, this is really going to be a gr-e-e-a-t Christmas!

(Lights out. All exit.)

Act II

SETTING: It is the following day. MARY is lying down in the middle of the living room floor with a pillow under her knees doing breathing exercises. JOSEPH is kneeling beside her and helping her as she breathes. The boxes of decorations have been removed from the chair.

DAVID *(enters from the right)*: Hi, guys! Whatcha' doin'?

JOSEPH: Practicing our breathing exercises for the birth.

DAVID *(goes over to them and kneels beside JOSEPH)*: You mean you have to breathe differently when the baby comes?

JOSEPH: Yeah. You see, David, there is some pain involved with the birth experience, but with proper breathing techniques, Mary can reduce the amount and intensity of the pain and keep somewhat relaxed.

DAVID: Hey, that's pretty neat! Sounds simple!

JOSEPH: That depends on a lot of things. Hey, we really appreciate your hospitality in putting us up for the night. It's too bad we missed our bus, but at least we had people like you to offer us shelter.

DAVID: No problem.

MARY: Your Dad seemed a little uptight about it.

DAVID: Oh, Dad was just caught off guard, that's all! Say, Joe, when's your bus leave?

JOSEPH: Five-twenty this afternoon. Is it going to be a problem for you to drive us to the station?

DAVID: Nah!

JOSEPH: If it is, we can always take a cab.

DAVID: Believe me, Joe. It's OK.

MARY: Sweetie, I'm getting pretty tired. I think I'll go lay down for a while.

JOSEPH: OK, honey. Let me help you up. *(He helps her to her feet.)* David, I think I'll lay down with Mary for a while.

DAVID: Sure. *(MARY and JOSEPH exit to the right. DAVID sits on couch. HENRY enters from left, wearing a jogging suit, and is panting.)* Dad, you still jog every day?

HENRY: Of course! Jogging is good for your heart. Helps you live longer. I've got to sit down. *(Sits in chair.)*

DAVID: Dad, I hope you're not too upset with me for bringing Joe and Mary home. They really did need a place to spend the night. After all, she is pregnant. I couldn't bear to think of their having to spend the whole night in the bus station.

HENRY: I suppose. I—I just wish you had let us know it before you brought them.

DAVID: Dad, if I had told you that I was bringing a pregnant woman and her husband home with me, you probably would have said "no way."

HENRY: I probably would have, but David, these two people are perfect strangers to you. I thought we had raised you to be more cautious with people you don't know at all.

DAVID: But Dad, I do know them. We had a great trip together on the bus from Roanoke.

HENRY: Great.

DAVID: They're real nice people. They are just trying to get to Mary's folks for the holidays, and they missed their bus.

HENRY: To where?

DAVID: Bethlehem.

HENRY: Bethlehem?

DAVID: Yes, Bethlehem, Pennsylvania.

HENRY: Figures.

DAVID: So anyway, Dad, I saw that they were in a tough spot, so I offered them a place to lay their heads last night. Now wasn't that the Christian thing to do?

HENRY: David, just because you're a Christian doesn't mean you open your home to every Tom, Dick, or—or Mary that comes along.

DAVID: I thought you once told me that the real meaning of Christmas is to give, not to receive, and you should give especially to those in need.

(STEPHANIE enters and hears the last part of the conversation.)

STEPHANIE: You said the same thing to me just last night, Dad.

HENRY: That was different.

DAVID: How?

HENRY *(paces back and forth a few steps)*: Well . . . well, it just was!

STEPHANIE: Come on, Dad. I want to hear some reasons.

HENRY: Well, I was talking about giving things to the City Mission or a turkey to a needy family. Things like that.

DAVID: Dad, there still isn't any difference. The only difference is that with this situation you can't just drop the turkey and run. You've got to be involved—to give for an extended period of time.

HENRY: But there is a difference. Sometimes people take advantage of you. They can see a sucker coming from a mile away. Who knows what these people are thinking?

STEPHANIE: Dad, I'm beginning to think all that stuff you fed me last night about "it's more blessed to give than to receive" is not true.

HENRY: You kids just don't understand.

DAVID: I understand clearly, Dad. The Christian thing to do is to help those in need, no matter if it's giving a turkey to a needy family or giving housing to a pregnant woman and her husband.

HENRY: But there's got to be a limit to what a person should do.

DAVID: Doesn't that make it pretty convenient for us?

HENRY: No—maybe—I don't know.

DAVID: Dad, to me, being a Christian means helping, regardless of the circumstances. It's giving ourselves in Christ's service. If I didn't believe that, I wouldn't have brought them home with me.

STEPHANIE: I think David's right. *(HENRY paces back and forth and then becomes thoughtful.)*

HENRY: Maybe so.

DAVID: I know what you're thinking, Dad. I thought the same thing when you used to make me share my ice cream cone with Steph.

HENRY: What do you mean?

DAVID: It's easy to have a giving heart as long as it's not you that has to give, but once that responsibility lands on your front doorstep, then it gets tough. How I hated to share my ice cream cone with Steph! I still do!

HENRY: Can a parent admit he's been wrong to the very kids he's been preaching to for all these years?

DAVID: It takes a real man to be able to do it.

STEPHANIE: We all make mistakes, Dad.

HENRY: I know, Steph. The problem is that I have been making too many.

DAVID: That's OK, Dad. In fact, it's probably great! Now you won't be nearly as mad when you see my grades for the first semester.

HENRY: What!!

DAVID: Just kidding, Dad. *(HELEN enters.)*

HELEN: Oh, there you are, Stephanie. Would you mind going to the store for me?

HENRY: I've got some shopping to do myself. How about if we go together, Steph?

STEPHANIE: Sure, Dad. *(They exit.)*

Act III

SETTING: The Brownstead living room, the afternoon of the same day. A few wrapped packages have been put under the tree. As the lights come on, MARY, JOSEPH, and DAVID enter from right. DAVID and JOSEPH each carry a suitcase.

DAVID: You guys really think you need to get to the bus station two hours ahead of time?

JOSEPH: Just to be safe, David. We don't want to miss another bus. And besides, we have to get our tickets.

MARY: We'll be OK, David.

DAVID: I know, but I just hate the thought of an expectant mother having to wait so long in a dirty old bus station.

JOSEPH: Hey, your station isn't so bad. You should see some of the other stations we've been to.

DAVID: Maybe someday I will. Well, I'll go get the car. *(Starts to exit left, as HENRY enters from left.)*

HENRY: Hi, Son. *(Looks at MARY and JOSEPH and their bags.)* You aren't leaving already, are you?

JOSEPH: Yes, sir. We thought we'd better get down to the station before the big rush for tickets.

HENRY: Well, listen. *(Walks over toward MARY and JOSEPH.)* Why doesn't David just drive you to Bethlehem?

JOSEPH: That's very nice of you to offer, Mr. Brownstead, but that would be too much. *(STEPHANIE enters from left.)*

HENRY: No, it wouldn't be too much.

JOSEPH: Yes, it would. That's 150 miles one way!

HENRY: So-o-o . . . I'd much rather have David drive you than to have him drop you off at that dirty old bus station.

DAVID: Dad, we were just talking about bus stations, and Joe says he's seen some that are a lot worse than ours!

HENRY *(ignores DAVID)*: Now let's have no arguing about it.

MARY: Excuse me, Mr. Brownstead. I don't want to seem ungrateful or anything, but why are you doing this? I mean, you don't know us from Adam and Eve. For all you know we might just be here because we think you're a sucker.

DAVID: Gee, it seems as if I heard someone else say that.

HENRY: We're doing it because we're Christians. We care about you. We want to help you.

JOSEPH: We always thought that kind of stuff was an act people put on. I mean, I hate to say it and everything, Mr. Brownstead, but we've had Christians tell us we need Jesus one minute and close the door in our faces the next. Granted, we're not the richest people on earth, but we're still people. We've tried hard, but haven't gotten the breaks.

HENRY: I hear what you're saying, Joe, but believe me, there are a lot of Christians out there who do care. We care and we want to help. Now go put your things in the car and stop refusing my offer.

JOSEPH *(turns to MARY)*: Well, what do you think?

MARY: I'm thinking that we need more people like the Brownsteads in this world.

JOSEPH: Me too!

STEPHANIE: Wait! Before you go, I want to give you something. *(She walks over to the Christmas tree and picks up a package and gives it to MARY.)*

MARY: What's this?

STEPHANIE: It's a couple of pairs of knee socks. Maybe you're like me and your feet get cold at night.

HENRY: Stephanie, how did you know they were—

STEPHANIE: Dad, I'll talk to you later.

MARY: Well, I don't know what to say!

STEPHANIE: You don't have to say anything.

DAVID: You know something. I have a present to give you also. Just a second! I'll go get it. *(He exits right.)*

JOSEPH: Does this kind of thing happen around here often?

HENRY: Only when we have visitors.

STEPHANIE: Who are on their way to Bethlehem.

MARY: Well, you sure are nice. *(HELEN enters with a container of cookies.)*

HELEN: Well, thank heavens you haven't left yet! I wanted to give you some of my Christmas cookies for the trip. *(Hands them to MARY.)*

MARY: Why, thank you, Mrs. Brownstead.

HELEN: My privilege, sweetie. There are Rudolphs and Santas and even some shepherds and camels.

MARY: Sounds like you've been busy.

HELEN: Yes, this is my last year doing it. *(DAVID enters from right.)*

DAVID *(carrying a quilt)*: Here you go. I want you to have this quilt that my grandmother gave me when I was born. You can lay the baby on it or wrap him in it, or whatever you like.

MARY: Thanks, David. Once again, I don't know what to say. We should be the ones giving you things.

JOSEPH: That's right. In fact, let me give you some money for last night's lodging. *(He reaches for his billfold.)*

HENRY: Keep your money, Joe. In fact, if you are ever in this area again, come and see us. *(He and JOSEPH shake hands.)* Now you'd better get going. The car is all gassed up and waiting.

JOSEPH: Thanks, everybody. This really will be a merry Christmas. Who knows, maybe Mary and I will even go to church on Christmas Eve.

HENRY: I hope so. *(Everyone exchanges good-byes. MARY leads the way as they exit to the left. JOSEPH and DAVID carry all the things out with them.)* You know, I think I'll write this story up and send it to the *Reader's Digest*.

STEPHANIE: Dad, you should wait awhile.

HENRY: How come?

STEPHANIE: Well, maybe they'll have a baby boy and name him Jesus.

HELEN: Stephanie, sometimes your imagination gets away from you! Have a boy and call him Jesus? Why there are probably thousands of

Joes and Marys married to each other. And I'm sure a number of them are expecting babies.

STEPHANIE: Yes, but how many of them are standing on doorsteps looking for a place to spend the night? *(Pause.)* You know what I think? I think they were sent here by God. That may sound strange, but that's how I feel. Dad, you had told me that the true meaning of Christmas is to give, not to receive, but I didn't believe you. Finally it hit me. When you and David had that discussion about what was the Christian thing to do, I saw you change from a father who was telling me what Christmas should be, to a father who told me what Christmas is. That means a lot to me, Dad. You know that checklist I made? *(HENRY nods.)* I tore it up and made a new one. The difference is that the new one is a list of things to give, not get.

HENRY: Steph, you're really growing up.

HELEN: Very fast.

HENRY: And you know something? I've been doing a lot of thinking myself.

HELEN: What are you cooking up now, Henry?

HENRY: Helen, today I went out and bought something. *(Exits to left.)*

HELEN: I hope it's not another birdbath.

STEPHANIE: Why would Dad go out and buy a birdbath on December 22?

HELEN: I don't know. Every time he says he's bought something I think of that ugly old birdbath in the backyard that he hates. I just know he's going to bring a new one home.

STEPHANIE: Mom, Dad hates birdbaths period!

HELEN: How do you know that?

STEPHANIE: He told me so. The only reason he puts up with that one is because he thinks you're in love with it. He hates having to mow the grass around it.

HELEN: Well, he never told. . . .

HENRY *(enters with a package)*: Well, here it is! *(All gather round as he opens the package.)*

HELEN: It's a Nativity set!

STEPHANIE *(picks up the Mary and Joseph figures)*: Hello, Mary and Joseph! I thought we just said good-bye to you!

HELEN: Why did you go out and buy these, Henry?

HENRY: Because I want to make sure that we never say good-bye to Mary and Joseph—not to the first Mary and Joseph or to our guests whose unexpected visit helped me to experience, for the first time in many years, the true meaning of Christmas.

STEPHANIE: Welcome to our family, Mary and Joseph!

A Bulletin Board for Advent— An Event

by Jane M. Grant

The display pictured here graphically portrayed the Advent theme "Peace on Earth" and was incorporated into one particular Advent worship service.

The worship service took the form of an agape meal or love feast, where food, praise, prayers, and hopes for worldwide peace were shared around tables set for family meals. At each individual's place was a strip of white paper. The directions on the strip of paper read:

1. Write your name on the white paper strip.
2. Eventually link your strip to the colorful paper chain on the bulletin board.

   The names of more than sixty locations of conflict areas in the world are written on the various links of the large chain. Please find a link representing an area of the world about which you are interested in learning more. At an appropriate time you will be asked to attach your personal link to the conflict area link you have chosen.
3. Hold this area in your prayerful concern during this season of peace.
   - Learn about the conflict area you have chosen.
   - Think about the people there.
   - Pray for the people there.
   - Pray for peace.

At the appropriate time worshipers of all ages were given the opportunity to attach their individual links to the linkage of humanity portrayed by the chain. The hope, of course, was to awaken a sense of spiritual oneness with all of God's children, for whom the Prince of Peace came. The serendipitous discovery was that church members often had to "link up" with one another to achieve linkage on the larger chain.

The completion of the peace chain bulletin board at the agape meal was the result of multigenerational participation and the culmination of previous interactions in the church family. The preparation for the bulletin board was an important part of an earlier Advent event.

A family night, the purpose of which was to ready the church building for the season, provided activities suitable for all ages. One of these was making the colorful chain to be strung across the map. Even very young children worked on the construction of the chain while older ones printed the names of the countries and regions experiencing political turmoil. Adults lent a hand in stringing up the chain.

The making of the huge map was a more difficult process; it could be done by youth or adults. A small map of the basic continental shapes was traced from an atlas onto a sheet of clear acetate.

A PEACE CHAIN

Link yourself in LOVE with your brothers and sisters around the world

Jane Grant

The resulting map was placed on an overhead projector, and the projected, enlarged image was drawn onto butcher paper. (Sheets of newspaper or a blank wall could also be used.) Our map measured four feet by nine feet.

This bulletin board remained posted for many weeks as a testimony to the prayer and outreach commitments made on that one Sunday in Advent. It involved all ages in its construction and in worship. As such it was different from the typical display board which is viewed passively.

Best of all, because a bulletin board can be seen and a prayer cannot, it became a visible and understandable expression of Christian community for children, visitors, and church members not present on that particular Advent Sunday.

Because of the amount of time invested in making the enlarged world map, it would be a good idea to recycle it from time to time. Another year the map could become the focus of a giving project. Replace the paper chain with a clothesline on which socks and mittens are attached with clothespins. "Encircle the world with gifts of love" would be an appropriate caption.

The map could also be used for mission education. Post on the map pictures of missionaries serving in various countries with a title such as "Faces and Places."

Celebrating Advent Across the Generations

by Thomas G. Bayes, Jr.

During Advent our Sunday church school becomes intergenerational. Persons of all ages meet together for the four Sundays. What follows is the program we used during one Advent season.

The First Sunday: "Prepare to Welcome Jesus"

Greeted with the sounds of a brass choir, everyone gathered to sing carols. Children were taught the first verses of "The Friendly Beasts." Leaders for the morning welcomed everyone: "Christmas comes again this year. It is coming, ready or not. He's the one for whom we have no room, not then, not now, not ever, until we take his Advent seriously."[1]

A man portraying the prophet Isaiah emerged from the crowd to share his experiences as prophet to King Ahaz. He told us of God's promise: a deliverer who would come from the family tree of David.

Next, two families shared their Christmas traditions. A three-generation family described preparing a special meal for Christmas Day. The second family demonstrated a homemade Advent calendar with its many symbols collected during family travels. Then the two families assembled a stable to begin building a crèche.

The "Jesse Tree," a large tree decorated with symbols portraying the spiritual heritage of Jesus, was a highlight of each Sunday. It traced the lineage of Jesus to David and was based on the words of the prophet Isaiah: "There shall come forth a shoot from the stump of Jesse [David's father]" (Isaiah 11:1). We decorated our Jesse Tree with a symbol for *each day* of Advent. On the back of each symbol was a biblical reading, an explanation, and a question for at-home family study. Seven sym-

bols for the first week of Advent were introduced. Our learning activity centered on coloring and mounting the symbols as decorations for our Jesse Tree and peoples' trees at home. At the end of the hour the lights were turned off and the Jesse Tree lighted; as each symbol was explained, a person placed it on the tree. With great joy we sang "Prepare Ye the Way of the Lord."

The Second Sunday: "Prepare to Give of Yourself"

People arrived to hear the handbell choir ringing Christmas carols. The theme was "In the final analysis you are the gift. That is why the birth of Jesus is so powerfully important. His coming to earth brought the reassurance of our worth as individual persons. He found us worthy of great gifts. He honored us. You are loved and lovable and worthy. And the gift of you, your love, is precious."[2]

---

[1]Wayne Saffer, *The First Season* (Minneapolis: Augsburg Fortress Publishers, 1973).

[2]Clyde Reid, *You Can Choose Christmas* (Waco, Tex.: Word Books, Inc., 1976).

The prophet Isaiah continued his story, telling how he gave Ahaz a sign from God that "a young woman shall conceive and bear a son and shall call his name Immanuel" (Isaiah 7:14). Two family traditions related to giving were shared. One family described "gift giving with coupons" that they create and present to one another. Mother read hers: "To Mom, one month of vacuuming!" The other family had baked a birthday cake for baby Jesus. Everyone joined in singing "Happy Birthday, Jesus," and cake was shared with the children. The two families added a manger to the stable.

Learning activities included completing seven more Jesse Tree symbols and making wrapping paper to wrap gifts for a children's center and for the jail. We concluded by hanging symbols on the Jesse Tree and singing "O Come, O Come, Emmanuel."

The Third Sunday: "Prepare to Receive the Gift of God"

A woodwind quintet with its lovely music helped continue our thoughtful preparation to receive God's gift. We were reminded of our difficulty in accepting gifts: "You shouldn't have"; "it's lovely but the wrong size"; or the bare response "thank you . . . what did you get?"[3] We need to learn how to accept God's gift to us in this season.

Another person spoke as the prophet Second Isaiah, who addressed Israel during the Exile and sought to reignite the spirits of his people, to prepare for the coming of God into their lives.

Two more family traditions were shared, and the two families added animals to our crèche as the children sang "The Friendly Beasts." Along with making symbols for the Jesse Tree, we made Christmas cards for people "who really needed to be appreciated."

The Fourth Sunday: "Prepare to Celebrate"

On this day our college students who had returned home and others brought their musical instruments to play in our "Advent Impromptu Band." We finished the Jesse Tree symbols, decorated Christmas cookies for the residents of the county jail, and completed our crèche. We were ready for Christmas!

The familiar words of Matthew and Luke were read: the stories of the shepherds and the kings. We watched Mary and Joseph (portrayed by two members) leave from the Jesse Tree and move toward the manger at the recitation of the words "There shall come forth a shoot from the stump of Jesse." In the darkened room Mary and Joseph lighted a single candle and placed it in the manger as this story was read:

A young man once dreamed that he held an unlit candle in his hand. Nearby, Jesus stood with a candelabra. The young man moved forward and Jesus lit his candle with his own. As the young man moved off into the darkness with his newly lit candle, eager to share his new light, his own breath blew out the flame. The young man turned back to see Jesus still standing there, holding the light. He returned hesitantly and held out his candle a second time. The Christ merely lit the young man's candle. Again his breath blew out the flame. Again he looked back, expecting some reproach; none came. Once more the Master relit his extinguished candle. Once more he started out. This pattern was repeated, but the young man noticed one thing. Each time he had gone farther before he lost his flame. With a lighter heart he returned once more to the Source, and once more he started out into the darkness.

Mary and Joseph took the light from the manger and lighted the candles of some persons seated near the stable, who then turned and shared their light with others. Soon the room was aglow with light from the "manger in Bethlehem." "Silent Night" was sung softly, and then triumphantly we sang "Joy to the World" to conclude our Advent celebration.

[3]Ibid.

Counting the Weeks Until Christmas

by Shirley Myers

After Thanksgiving is over, children look forward to Christmas. Recognizing their mounting excitement week by week is possible through the use of an Advent calendar. Here are three calendar ideas to mark the weekly progress of the Advent season with kindergarten and early elementary children.

Allow children to help in the construction of the section for each Sunday. When each section is complete, gather the children to hear the special Advent thought for that Sunday. You may read it to the children, or choose a different child each week to read the Advent thought.

Christmas Tree Advent Calendar

Make a Christmas tree in four sections out of green construction paper. Mount one section each week on a sheet of white poster board. Illustration A will show you the arrangement of the four sections. The tree may be any size that is adaptable for your use. If you wish, you may help the children construct small individual versions. Invite the children to make paper decorations for each section of the tree. They may design their own creations or cut pictures from old Christmas cards. You may wish to have the children glue on such things as sequins or rickrack.

Illustration A

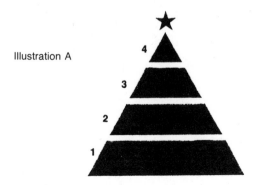

Advent Thoughts for Christmas Tree Calendar

1. Waiting for Christmas. Getting ready for Christmas is a lot of fun. Putting up the Christmas tree is a special time in most families. We move some of the furniture in our homes to make a place for it. We go to the attic and bring out decorations that are family treasures. We may buy or make some new treasures. The Christmas tree adds to the excitement of looking forward to Christmas. Long ago, prophets told their listeners that Jesus would be born. Two people who believed them were Simeon and Anna. They waited and waited. They never gave up. Every day they looked forward to the special day when Jesus would be born (Luke 2:22–38).

2. The Beauty of Christmas. Christmas is a time of beauty. That is why we try to make everything beautiful for Christmas. We put lights on the tree to make it bright. We add decorations to the tree. We put candles or wreaths in the windows.

Before Jesus was born, the world was a dreary place. People did not know where to look for hope. Jesus came to brighten the world with his beauty. The world has never been the same since Jesus came. Jesus taught people to have hope. They make the world a better place when they live by his teachings.

3. The Joy of Christmas. One of the signs that Christmas is near is the singing of special Christmas songs. We hear them on the radio and in the stores. Choirs sing the songs of Christmas. Families often gather around or near the Christmas tree to sing.

Christmas songs are songs of joy. They tell the story of Christmas and help us to be happy that Jesus came.

4. The Best Christmas Gift. Have you put up

the Christmas tree at your house? Are there any gifts under the tree yet? Or does your family wait until Christmas Eve to put the gifts under the tree? It is fun to see other people's happiness when we give them gifts. It is also fun to receive a gift.

We have all received one gift that makes us very happy. God gave Jesus as a Christmas gift to the world. Jesus brings us the true joy and happiness of Christmas. (If the children know John 3:16, they may say it at this point, or one or all of the children may find it in the Bible and read it.)

Candle Advent Calendar

For this Advent calendar activity, you will need four sheets of medium-blue construction paper (large or small) and several narrow strips of white construction paper. Arrange the blue paper to form windows according to Illustration B or C. Use the white paper strips to form a frame around each window. On each Sunday of Advent you will add a paper candle and a particular word to one of the four windows. Have the candleholders, candles, and flames already cut out of construction paper. To give the impression of the light or aura around the flames, cut circles from aluminum foil and place them behind the flames. Imprint the words on the foil with a blunt pencil. (See Illustration D.)

Invite different children each week to tape or paste these parts in a window.

Advent Thoughts for Candle Calendar

1. Hope. As evening came on, threatening clouds moved across the sky. The wind blew. The lightning began to flash. Thunder rumbled and roared. Flash! Clap! Flash! Clap! Then all the lights went out. We stumbled through the house to find a candle and a match. The light of the candle made a warm glow in the room. What a change! Right away everyone felt better. Jesus is called the light of the world. The world became a different place when he came. People had been unhappy. They were waiting for a change. The kings and rulers were mean. The people had not obeyed God. They did not know what to do to feel good about life. When Jesus came, everything seemed brighter. People now had hope.

2. Love. Jesus was born to show us God's love. At Christmastime we celebrate God's love, which forgives us. People who believe in Jesus can draw close to God. We know that God's love is always with us.

3. Give. Giving is what Christmas is all about! It began with God's gift of Jesus to the world. The wise men gave gifts to the special baby. The man Jesus gave his life for his followers. We celebrate Jesus' birth by giving gifts to those we love. We

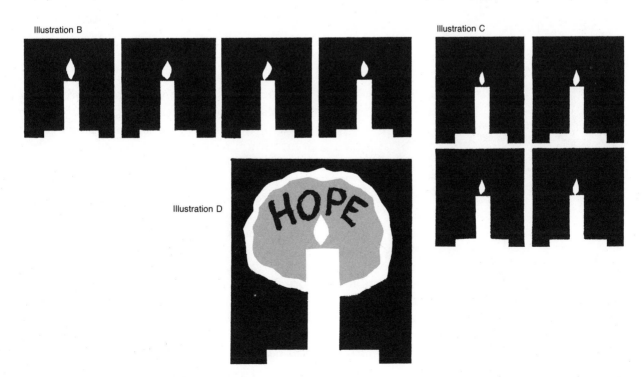

Illustration B

Illustration C

Illustration D

can also give gifts to people we don't even know—lonely, homeless, hungry persons. Buying a gift is not the only way to give! We may give the gift of a visit or do an errand. We can give outgrown clothes and toys in good condition. We can make gifts such as tree ornaments or cookies. In whatever ways you give, remember to give thanks for God's gift of Jesus.

4. Everyone. Jesus was born in a little town, but he came to the whole world. Everyone can be part of God's family. The story of the wise men who came to worship Jesus reminds us of the people in all parts of the world who worship Jesus. The wise men followed the light of a special star. So, when we see the Christmas lights, we can think of people everywhere who believe in Jesus.

Nativity Scene Advent Calendar

To make an Advent calendar that shows the Nativity, you will need a sheet of poster board in your choice of color and construction paper in a variety of colors. For the first week of Advent you will need enough strips of brown construction paper to outline the stable on poster board as in Illustration E.

Illustration E

For the second week you will need to make simple figures of a sheep and a donkey out of brown and gray construction paper. Using colors of your choice, make simple figures of Mary and Joseph for the third week. If you cannot draw the figures, you may cut what you need from Christmas cards or outdated curriculum. For the fourth week, make a manger bed and a baby.

On the first Sunday of Advent, put the stable in place but keep the other items in a see-through bag nearby so that the children will continue anticipating the completion of the scene. Invite the children to paste the figures in the stable in the following weeks of Advent. See Illustration F.

A variation of this activity could be done on a flannel board. This would make it possible to take the pictures down so that several children could arrange and rearrange them.

Illustration F

Advent Thoughts for Nativity Scene

1. No room in the inn. If you and your family were going on a long trip, how would you travel? Would you walk? Would you ride on a donkey? No, you would probably ride in a comfortable car. Perhaps you might even travel by bus or train or plane. When your trip was over, you would go to a nice warm room with a soft bed, and there you would rest. This room might be in a hotel or a relative's home where there were many other things to make you comfortable.

When Mary and Joseph traveled sixty or seventy miles from Nazareth to Bethlehem, they did not have an easy trip. There was no comfortable car or train or plane to get them there quickly! Joseph walked as he led the donkey on which Mary rode. Joseph wanted to take good care of Mary. He loved her, and she was going to have a baby very soon. He thought about the dream he had had. In the dream an angel had told him that the baby would be special.

Mary longed for a nice quiet room where she could rest when the journey was over. What a disappointment it was to find that there were no empty rooms in the hotel in Bethlehem! All they could do was rest in the stable where the animals were kept.

2. Animals for roommates. Do you have any animals in your room at home? Maybe your pet cat or dog sometimes sleeps with you. Or perhaps you have some stuffed animals on your bed. But do you have a cow or donkey in your room? No, of course not. Those animals belong in the barn or stable. Mary and Joseph were in the stable with the animals after their long trip. There were probably sheep and maybe a donkey. In the moonlight the animals looked harmless, but they didn't smell very good. They were quiet, but now and then they made noises as they ate out of the food box called a manger. The stable was not the nicest place to sleep, but it was the only place that Mary and Joseph could spend the night.

3. Waiting for the birth. Mary and Joseph looked around. There were no other people; only the animals were nearby. Mary and Joseph tried to sleep, but they were too excited. Mary could tell that it was almost time for her baby to be born. They talked about what they would name the baby and what the next few days would be like.

4. Born in a barn. Do you know where you were born? Most children are born in hospitals, and some are born at home. But I know only one person who was born in a barn. Guess who? Here's a clue: the baby was a boy, and his mother's name was Mary. Yes, it was Jesus.

What a baby! All babies are lovable, but this child, Jesus, was born for a special reason. He came to show God's love to the world. He came so that we could know God and learn how to live right. What a special baby he was! As Mary and Joseph looked down at the new baby, they remembered the words of the angel, "You shall call his name Jesus, for he will save his people from their sins" (Matthew 1:21).

Does Santa Belong in Church?

Rediscovering the Feast Day of Nicholas of Myra

by Robert S. Reid

How should churches respond to the whole Santa Claus tradition? One member of my parish recently remarked, "Oh, he was banned around here a long time ago." Yet, on the same day I read in the newsletter of one of our sister congregations an announcement of the annual Christmas party for children with a visit from "you know who." Is it really an all-or-nothing tradition?

When my family decided that neither giving in nor withdrawing was the best response, we did some spadework on good old Saint Nick. The result was our discovery of the Feast Day of Saint Nicholas. The original story of Bishop Nicholas of Myra and his gracious acts of mercy lies at the heart of much of our Christmas tradition. Our family became convinced that sharing our "stocking gifts" on his real feast day was an effective way to positively defuse the "Christmas machine." We were able to establish the true story of Santa Claus and joyously allow our children to understand how one act of mercy has tumbled down through the centuries in a joyous tale of a cherry-cheeked old elf. The Feast Day of Nicholas of Myra is now a wonder-filled portion of our Advent celebration.

Part of our task in ministry is to find creative ways to help families in our churches recover the sense that it really can be a "blessed season." For many Christian teachers and parents, the question seems to be how best to respond to the ever-present Santa Claus. Jolly Old Saint Nicholas seems to possess an invincible durability that can outlast even the toughest jeers of our jaded peers. Somehow this venerable old saint still manages to embody the mirth and good tidings of the Christmas season and to dominate what most of our school districts now must call the winter program.

Celebrate the Feast Day of Nicholas of Myra

As church teachers and leaders search for creative ways to add new vitality to their Advent celebration, the Feast Day of Nicholas of Myra can provide a unique opportunity. A congregation and its families may be able to reclaim the best part of Saint Nick's charm before he gets completely lost in the trail of his heavenly host of "eight tiny reindeer."

For centuries the Christian church has celebrated Saint Nicholas's day on December 6, a day that falls reasonably early in the traditional Advent celebration. Nestled far enough past Thanksgiving to allow stout-hearted workers to marshall

their forces, this date still permits parents and teachers to have a solid lead on the momentum that builds toward the fateful night of "dancing sugarplums." It may also allow many children, families, and teachers an opportunity to regain some of the joy of stocking gifts that are so often dwarfed by the brightly bundled boxes that engulf our trees.

But why should we reinstate the celebration of a feast day for Nicholas of Myra? To get beneath the layers of tradition of that "right jolly old elf," we need to rediscover the story of this patron saint of children, a story that has demonstrated an amazing resilience as it has come to us down through the centuries.

Bishop Nicholas of Myra

Surviving Byzantine carvings and paintings help us to uncover Nicholas's popular trail. His image was occasionally thin and forbidding, while at other times he was depicted as splendidly robed with a glorious bishop's mitre and scepter. By the twelfth century his popularity was so great that he stood third in line following Jesus and Mary as the recipient of the hopes and prayers of the common people. The Protestant reformers vigorously tried to eliminate his "cult," for by that time the line between the worship of God and the veneration of the saints had virtually collapsed. But Nicholas of Myra had a tenacity that even Luther could not chase out of the German heritage.

The actual Nicholas appears to have been born in Patara, now part of modern-day Turkey, possibly in the year A.D. 280. He eventually became the bishop of the town of Myra, a coastal Mediterranean village. He appears to have been one of more than three hundred participating church leaders at the First Council of Nicea in A.D. 325. But tradition could not allow Nicholas merely to attend. As Arius (a cleric who was denounced as a heretic) spoke, Nicholas is said to have been so outraged by the heresy being presented that he walked up to the speaker and struck him across the face. This audacious action was supposedly vindicated by a private visitation of the risen Lord and his mother. It was the testimony of that vision that was said to have swayed the vote of the council against Arius.

Sainthood is built on authenticating miracles, and many stories flourished. Nicholas eventually became known as the saint who was always ready to help wherever need existed. Through several stories of miraculous deliverances, he became known throughout eastern Europe as the patron saint of sailors.

Yet, under all the trappings of legends comes the simple tale of a pastor who once helped a poor man to marry off each of his three daughters. Each time the family thought all was lost because of not having a dowry for the bride-to-be, the pastor secretly passed a stocking filled with three hundred florins through the window. Unmasked during his third mission of mercy, Saint Nicholas was respected in silence throughout his life. Then, as so often happens when good and honorable people are venerated after their death, this one disarming anecdote inspired many stories of miraculous occurrences. One such tale, which involved the resurrection of three children who had been gruesomely killed, established Nicholas as the patron saint of all children.

Saint Nicholas in the New World

Curiously enough it was his dual role as patron saint of sailors and children that eventually inspired some citizens of New York City to add some color to their own limited heritage in the New World. One of our country's first noted literary works is the fancifully concocted *Dietrich Knickerbocker's History of New York from the Beginning of the World to the End of the Dutch Dynasty* by Washington Irving. In a crucial portion in the history of the founding of New York, one of the characters describes a dream in which the bust of Saint Nicholas leaves its carved post on the bow of the ship to make generous provision in picking just the right site for the Dutch settlers in founding their town. Thus begins the tale of Saint Nicholas's relationship as the patron saint of New York. Yet this particular Saint Nicholas has none of the demeanor of the ancient bishop of Myra. Instead, he sounds suspiciously like a pipe-smoking, rosy-cheeked Dutchman.

A second New Yorker, Clement Clarke Moore, drew upon this image when he penned a delightful poem to be read to his daughters and a few guests on the evening of December 23, 1822. Moore was a leading Hebrew scholar and one of the founding faculty of the General Theological Seminary of New York. He enjoyed writing verse as a hobby. Clement Moore could hardly have guessed that he would be forever immortalized by creating a small flight of fancy that began, " 'Twas the night before Christmas. . . ."

Within a few decades the New York artist Thomas Nast completed the reformulation of Saint Nicholas by visually creating the character described in Moore's inimitable poem. Nast drew his now famous depiction of Saint Nicholas with thoughtful recreations of images of his boyhood in Bavaria with its observance of lighted festival trees to celebrate the Christmas season. Much of the raw material for the Santa Claus legend is quite Christian and European, but the final creation is a uniquely American product of the city of New York.

So Nicholas of Myra evolved into Santa Claus because times and needs change. Previous generations desired a patron saint of protection. Our age, on the other hand, seems to yearn for the spirit of altruism embodied in a kindly father figure who cares for children of all generations. He has become someone who graciously, generously, and secretly provides for us at the time we need him. Legends lent his name to a multitude of needs, but at its heart his story tells of how mercy overcomes circumstances.

Meanings for Today

For young minds Nicholas of Myra's story can effectively convey the message of Advent—God's mercy and provision unwrapped in the face of judgment. His traditional feast day is a day to fill stockings with mercy just as Nicholas had once provided another family with merciful provision. Even Clement Moore's Saint Nicholas silently filled the children's stockings with gifts.

The tradition of small gifts placed in hanging stockings seems to be passing away. Our Christmas present extravaganzas overshadow most of the "stocking stuffers." Yet, it is the stocking part of Christmas that is most traditionally associated with Saint Nicholas and his act of mercy toward others. With all its humility, the stocking could be recovered as part of the real meaning of Christmas gift giving in our Advent celebration.

Using the Message of Saint Nicholas

In the Church School

If handled with sensitivity and the proper preparation, the true story of Santa Claus can be told as an example of a person of Christ who acted in love

to provide for others. The wise teacher would want to alert parents that talking about Santa would be part of the Sunday church school session on a certain date. When the material is presented as an attempt to reclaim our true heritage for the education and enjoyment of our children, we can begin to transcend the polarized reactions of "giving in" to Santa Claus or "saying nothing"—the two reactions that seem to characterize many of our churches and their Sunday church schools.

By seeing an analogy between Saint Nicholas's secret gift to the poor and God being "secreted" into the world in the coming of Christ, older children can make the association between the observance of Saint Nicholas's act of mercy and love and that of God in Christ.

Children can be encouraged to think about ways that they might help others who have needs as a symbol of the mercy that God expressed in sending Jesus Christ into the world and as a symbol of the mercy that Nicholas of Myra expressed when he provided the money for the dowries of each of the three daughters. The class might collect food or presents to give to organizations that help others in the tradition of Nicholas of Myra.

Children could suggest several practical projects of giving in which they could act with the same love and mercy that Saint Nicholas demonstrated.

The class might be highly stimulated if three separate "stockings of mercy" were quite suddenly cast secretly into the room during the practical project time. Rather than "goodies," the stockings might contain those things that could be merciful provisions for a needy person. The "stocking of mercy" cast into the room may prompt discussion about who might need the kind of mercy expressed by the contents of the stocking.

In the Worship Service or Advent Program

After some of the tradition is conveyed, members of the congregation could be encouraged to participate in a "stockings of mercy" or "stockings of sharing" campaign. The stockings would be given to needy people in the name of Nicholas of Myra who served the Lord of Christmas.

The story of Saint Nicholas could be shared during the lighting of the second Advent candle.

In the Home

Families could be encouraged to observe the Feast Day of Nicholas of Myra as part of the home

Advent celebration. Churches could provide materials to help parents effectively share his story and the relationship of this godly person to Santa Claus.

Simple stockings of mercy could be shared at this time of the Christmas season rather than on December 25. Small stocking stuffers could provide a wonderful opportunity to reclaim our own heritage.

Special reading of joyful stories about Saint Nicholas, both factual and fanciful, could enhance the learning experience and the family time during this festive day. Information can be found in such resources as Harold Myra's excellent retelling of the Saint Nicholas story in *Santa, Are You for Real?* (Nashville: Thomas Nelson Inc., 1977) and short readings such as Clement Clarke Moore's *"'Twas the Night Before Christmas"* or the widely anthologized editor's response in the September 21, 1897, edition of the *New York Sun* entitled "Yes, Virginia, There Is a Santa Claus."

Family members could give other family members mercy presents—that time, thing, or experience that would show mercy during the Christmas season.

The feast day could involve a "Myra dinner," an occasion when new friends could be invited to share in the gift of hospitality and friendship.

This year rather than merely decrying the commercialization of the season, take time early in Advent to form the kind of church and family traditions that will reclaim the joy of giving as part of Advent.

Resources

Best of Christmas Joys, by Joan Winmill Brown. New York: Doubleday Publishing Co., 1983.

Saint Nicholas: Life and Legend, by Martin Ebon. New York: Harper & Row, Publishers Inc., 1975.

The Oxford Dictionary of the Christian Church, by F. L. Cross and Elizabeth Livingstone. New York: Oxford University Press Inc., 1974.

Some of these resources may be available at the public library; if not, the library will have something similar.

Christmas Cloth

A Celebration for Christmas

by John Brown

This program can be used either as a time for intimate worship among members of a youth or adult group or for a wider church Christmas celebration.

Contrary to popular belief, Christmas is not the high point of the Christian calendar. Since early times, Lent and Easter have been dominant in Christian liturgy. Christmas is a beginning, but the apex of Christian faith is in the empty tomb. The events of Jesus' life led up to the resurrection.

This program reviews Jesus' life as symbolized by the clothes mentioned in Scripture—the infant clothes, the hem of his garment touched by a woman during his ministry, the robe that was gambled away at his death, and the grave cloths, symbol of the living Lord.

Preparation

Make this a time of good fellowship and singing. Use Christmas carols liberally throughout the service. Carols are suggested here, but use some other hymns as well as solos or special Christmas music. Although we will be considering various aspects

Providence Lithograph

of Jesus' life, Christmas music is appropriate. It is fitting at any time of the year!

You may want to use the *Good News Bible* or another contemporary translation for the Scripture readings.

If you are using this material in a small group, arrange seating in a circle or semicircle around the Christmas candles, a small tree, or a display of Christmas art. Spoken parts can be given from within the circle.

If this material is to be used as a part of a wider Christmas celebration in a church sanctuary or meeting hall, consider using two lecterns, one for the Scripture readings and one for voice parts.

The Experience

Carol: "Away in a Manger"

Scripture: Luke 2:1–7 (All Scripture is GNB.)

Reading: "Baby Clothes"

Christmas is a high point in the Christian year. We celebrate the birth of Jesus, God in person, who lived and lives among us. But Christmas is a beginning, a starting point. The manger is linked to the empty tomb. Without the resurrection Jesus would be only a kind man, a good man, a prophet, an example, a great philosopher along with other great personalities of history. But he was very God—in diapers and baby clothes! He said he came to earth to redeem us and to give us hope for life after life. As a seal or verification of who he was, his life led to an early and untimely death and to victory over death.

We are contemplating his clothes, the garments that he wore. He started out in baby clothes or swaddling cloths—simple pieces of cloth in which Mary wrapped him.

Billions of babies have been born through the

centuries of time. Most were tenderly loved and cared for by their mothers and dressed in infants' apparel. A baby is a helpless person, totally dependent on someone else. Most creatures of our world at least can stand or walk or feed themselves at birth. Not so the human creature. It is usually at least a year before a child can stand, walk, and begin to learn the rudiments of feeding and caring for itself. Total dependency!

And God chose to visit us in person and to become, for a time, totally dependent and trusting in the love and faithfulness of parents. We speak of trust in God! See how he trusted us! He could not even clothe himself. His mother had to do it for him—in baby clothes—in a manger.

Carol: "Angels We Have Heard on High"

Scripture: Matthew 9:20–22

Reading: "The Edge of His Cloak"

And the child grew and developed with the loving nurture given him by Mary and Joseph. Then when he was fully grown, he began doing amazing things, marvelous things, disturbing things, dangerous things, threatening things. He began to spread news—Good News—that God had come to release people from the chains, burdens, and consequences of sin, fear, and guilt. He dared to forgive sins! He dared to cure sickness, even on the sabbath! He dared to promise abundant life in a forsaken, downtrodden, despairing world!

He roamed the countryside with poor people and outcasts, camping out, laughing and celebrating, teaching and reasoning, tending to the sick and disabled. He lived life to its fullest and was weary and exhausted night after night from work and rejoicing and discussions long into the night.

We do not know just what he wore during those brief years—a cloak, a robe, a garment. But on one of his journeys a woman—any woman—felt the need for healing. Not only did she feel the need, but she also acted. She did not set up an appointment for counseling or a doctor's examination. She crept up behind Jesus, reached out, and touched his cloak.

There was no magic in the cloth. It was her reaching out and his accepting her act that made the difference. Jesus didn't even take credit for healing, for locked up inside this woman was the cure for her own ills—her faith. Note what he said to her, "Your faith has made you well."

Lord, how often we are afraid to reach out to another person or to you! We fear rejection or embarrassment. We are too proud to admit need. Give us confidence and courage to reach out to you with assurance that you will stop, pay attention, and help us. Help us to reach out to others as well and to accept those who reach out for us. Lord God, we would but touch the edge of your cloak this Advent season. Amen.

Carol: "O Come, O Come, Emmanuel"

Scripture: John 19:23–24

Reading: "Gambled Garment"

He ended up without a penny. They didn't even allow him the dignity of his last earthly possession—the robe that he wore. As if torture, insult, and death weren't enough, they gambled away his garments.

He ministered to people and they murdered him. The cycle was complete—the cradle to the grave.

Or was it? Was it all without purpose? God has the strangest ways of turning darkness to day. His birth, his ministry, his death—all had meaning. The baby clothes, the cloak, the gambled robe—all led to a final, finer piece of cloth.

Carol: "Hark! The Herald Angels Sing"

Scripture: John 19:38–40; 20:3–8

Reading: "The Shroud"

It all seemed so useless, so tragically useless. A life so worthwhile, so beautiful—snuffed out by one of the most horrible deaths ever contrived.

But it was all over now. No more healing, no more Good News, no more late-night talks, no more bread for the hungry, no more rejoicing. The final chapter had been written to the life of a great person who never really made it. There were such high hopes, such dreams and plans.

It ended something like it began. He was lying down again; this time in a tomb, not a manger; not glowing with life, but stone dead; not dressed in baby clothes, but in a linen sheet and face cloth.

How could the Babe of Bethlehem, the man-

Providence Lithograph

ger child, end up in bloody grave cloths?

Then a spark more potent than a nuclear flash split the dawn. A rumor spread. He had risen from the dead!

Two disciples came running. They entered the tomb. They found nothing. Absolutely nothing! Nothing except a linen shroud and a face cloth that once covered a dead man.

He is risen! The Lord is risen indeed! This is not only the message of Easter, but also of Christmas. Christmas is the joyous celebration of baby clothes and a folded burial shroud. He came to bring hope, Good News, and the promise of life!

Prayer: O Lord, we are joyous at the Christmas season because you came in person to bring us redemption, to show us the way to walk in this world, and to give us the hope of life. Amen.

Carol: "Joy to the World" (Or consider using an Easter hymn as a fitting closing to this service.)

Reprinted from *Worship Celebrations for Youth,* by John Brown. Copyright © 1980, published by Judson Press. Used by permission of Judson Press.

Christmas—A Beginning and an Ending

by Lois A. Glading

Christmas had a creative beginning and a festive ending at our church. By using ideas we borrowed from others, we had two large and meaningful all-church celebrations.

Deck the Halls Night

Christmas began on a Friday evening in early December with "Deck the Halls" night. (A new member of our church had shared this idea with us based on an experience her family had enjoyed each year in a former church.) The purpose of the evening was to make decorations for a large church Christmas tree.

As people arrived that evening, they found seventeen different crafts set up—all tree decorations. The crafts ranged from very simple crafts for small children, to intermediate crafts, to more intricate crafts for adults. For ninety minutes persons of all ages decorated cookies, made paper chains, strung popcorn and cranberries, painted wooden ornaments, and created lambs, wreaths, and other decorations. As each ornament was finished, the individual's name was put on it, and then it was hung on the Christmas tree in "just the right spot." The result was a beautifully decorated tree, which at the beginning of the evening had had only lights on it.

After all that hard work and creativity, everyone was ready for refreshments. Refreshments were kept easy and simple. Each family brought one dozen of their favorite Christmas cookies and the recipe. The cookie recipes were placed on a poster board to be copied by those who wanted them. There were plenty of cookies for everyone to sample. Punch was provided by the board of Christian education.

Next on the agenda was a time to gather around the Christmas tree and sing carols with guitar accompaniment. The evening ended with the telling

of Barbara Robinson's Christmas classic, *The Best Christmas Pageant Ever* (New York: Avon Books, 1983).

All agreed it had been a beautiful way to begin the Christmas season. Expenses were minimal and were offset by a free-will offering.

Twelfth Night Celebration

Now that the tree was decorated, the question arose, "Who undecorates the tree?" The answer lay in a "Twelfth Night Celebration" on January 6. Our church had never celebrated Twelfth Night or Epiphany. Epiphany, at the conclusion of the twelve days of Christmas, is observed in the church year on January 6 as the time when the wise men came to see the baby Jesus. Custom also has it as the time to undecorate the Christmas tree, put away the decorations, and complete the Christmas celebration. Another custom is the serving of a Twelfth Night or Three Kings Cake. Recipes for the cake vary widely, but all recipes agree that a nut, bean, or silver coin is baked inside the cake. The lucky finder is then crowned king or queen for the evening. After a busy Christmas season of some other traditional events (the Christmas tea, choir cantata, and three candlelight Christmas Eve services), January 6 arrived. Children in grades 1–6 and several of their mothers were involved in planning and participating in the "Twelfth Night Celebration," which was originally described in *Pockets*.[1]

As people undecorated the Christmas tree, claiming the decorations they had made a month earlier, they enjoyed eating a piece of a "Delaware Twelfth Night Cake." Four cakes had been baked, with three of them containing one bean each.

Imagine our surprise when we crowned the bean finders—three queens, instead of kings! The queens, two five-year-old girls and an adult woman, were given seats of honor, and crowns were placed on their heads. The story from Matthew 2 of the coming of the wise men was read, and then the queen (and the congregation) were entertained. The children's and youth choirs sang. Several of our youth performed vocal and instrumental duets.

The evening ended with a Feast of Lights. As the room was darkened, the Christ candle was lit and John 1:1–18 was read. The three queens came forward to light their candles from the Christ candle, and then they shared the candlelight with all

who were present. Small individual candles had previously been distributed. As the candlelight was being spread about the room, all joined in singing several Christmas carols, beginning with "We Three Kings," for the last time this Christmas season. Prayer and a challenge to share the light of Christ with someone else during the new year concluded the "Twelfth Night Celebration."

Someone later expressed, "It was a beautiful way to neatly "tie up" the Christmas experience.

Delaware Twelfth Night Cake

In Sussex County, Delaware, a bounteous dinner marks Epiphany, featuring a Twelfth Night Cake in which a nut is hidden. The finder, it is said, will have good luck all the year. Here is a recipe based on some of the old Sussex ones and tested by *Woman's Day*.

2 cups (500 milliliters) butter, softened but not runny
2¼ cups (550 milliliters) sugar
8 large eggs, at room temperature
5 cups (1.25 liters) sifted cake flour, lightly spooned into cup
½ teaspoon (2.5 milliliters) salt
1 teaspoon (5 milliliters) nutmeg
3 teaspoons (15 milliliters) ginger
½ teaspoon (2.5 milliliters) mace
1 nut (or bean, or pure silver coin)

Cream butter and sugar until light. Add eggs, one at a time, beating well after each. Sift dry ingredients and add to mixture, stirring to blend. Before pouring into a greased and floured 10-inch (25-centimeter) tube pan, add the nut and stir to hide the nut in the mixture. Bake in a slow oven, 275° (135°C), for 2 to 2½ hours.

Turn out on rack; cool.

---

[1]*Pockets* is a monthly Christian magazine for elementary children. It may be ordered from the publisher: The Upper Room, 1908 Grand Ave., P.O. Box 189, Nashville, TN 37202.